IRISH SOLDIERS IN COLONIAL AMERICA
(ca.1650-1825)

By
David Dobson

CLEARFIELD

Copyright © 2023
by David Dobson
All Rights Reserved

Published for Clearfield Company by
Genealogical Publishing Company
Baltimore, Maryland
2023

ISBN: 9780806359588

Introduction to Irish Soldiers in Colonial America

This volume attempts to identify many of the Irish soldiers in the British colonies in North America and the Caribbean from around 1650 until 1825.

Before 1800 Ireland was a separate kingdom but subject to the British king. The last king of Ireland was the Catholic King James II who encouraged the formation of Irish regiments, such as the Royal Irish Regiment from 1684, Royal Irish Dragoon Guards from 1685, 27th Inniskilling Foot from 1689, Royal Irish Lancers from 1689, and Inniskilling Dragoons from 1689. After James' defeat at the Battle of the Boyne in 1690 most of his forces, thought to be around 2,000 men, crossed over to France, in what is known as the 'Flight of the Wild Geese,' where they formed regiments in the French Army such as Montcashel's, O'Brian's, and Dillon's.

Irish soldiers fought in various campaigns in Europe and in Canada, and probably the Caribbean, until the French Revolution when they were disbanded. The British Army did not enlist Irish Catholics during much of the eighteenth century as they were considered likely to be unreliable when they opposed the forces of Catholic countries such as France and Spain, which contained many of their countrymen. Ireland was garrisoned mainly by British regiments, though new regiments were raised in Ireland, such as The Royal Regiment of Foot of Ireland and the Inniskilling Regiment. Initially regiments were known by the surname of their Colonel, but in 1751 the British Army introduced the use of numbers in regimental titles; thus Blakeney's Regiment became the 23rd Regiment of Foot.

Irish settlers, including those exiled to British colonies, were recruited into local militias, such as the Virginia Regiment or the Montserrat Militia, which are identified in this book. During the American Revolution people of Irish origin could be found in both Loyalist and Patriot units, including the 'Volunteers of Ireland'. The Loyalist Claims proved very useful in identifying Irish fighting men. Between 1789 and 1815 Britain was at war with Napoleon's France, necessitating an expansion of the British Army. In the aftermath of the Battle of Waterloo the British government settled substantial numbers of demobilised soldiers, including Irishmen, in Canada. From about 1780 onwards the British regiments enlisted at least one-third of their recruits in Ireland; this increased to about 40% by the early nineteenth century owing to demand from the British Army and the East India Company.

For additional information about Irish recruits that served in the Colonies, see 'A Historical Record of the 27th [Inniskilling] Regiment', by W C Trimble, [1851]; Richard Cannon's 'Historical record of the 18th [Royal Irish] Regiment of Foot', [London 1848]; and Steven M Baule's 'Protecting the Empire's Frontier, Officers of the 18th [Royal Irish] Foot', [Ohio, 2013]; as well as the journals of the Army Historical Research Society, and those of the 'Irish Sword'.

David Dobson, Dundee, Scotland, 2023

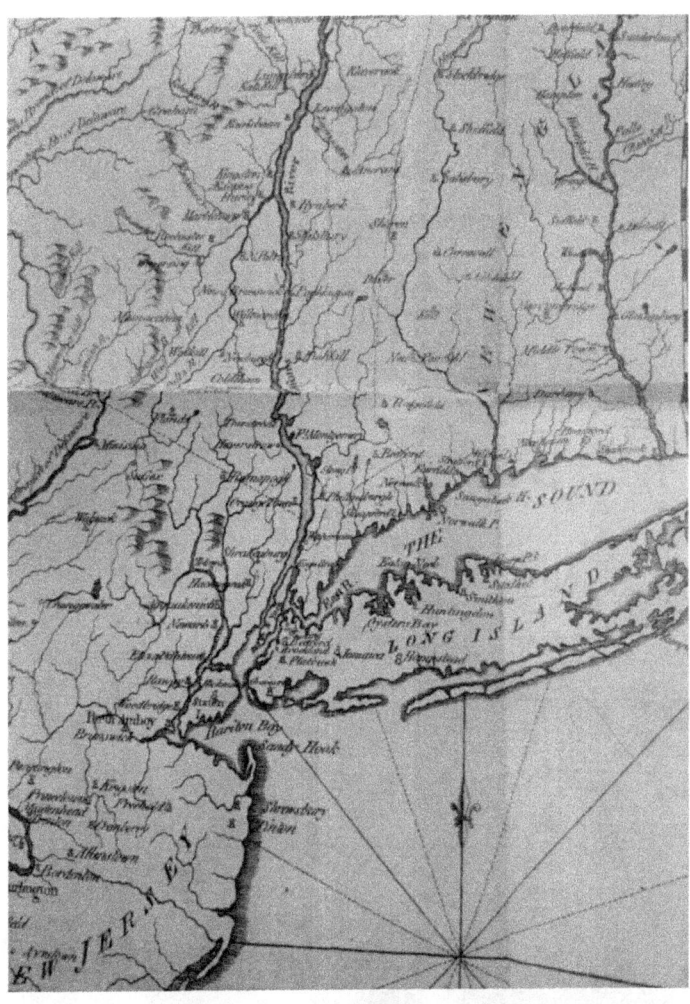

Map of parts of colonial New York, New Jersey, and Connecticut

Irish soldiers in Caribbean uniforms

Inniskilling soldier from 1680

An officer of the 6th (Inniskilling) Dragoons, 1811

IRISH SOLDIERS IN COLONIAL AMERICA

ADAIR, ROBERT, a soldier of the 18th [Royal Regiment of Ireland] Foot, in Philadelphia, Pennsylvania, in 1770, as transferred on 9 October 1774 in New York. [TNA.WO.76/25]

ADAIR, ..., Surgeon General to the Army, reference 10 July 1782. [HMC.American.iii.15]

ADAMS, Sergeant JAMES, in Montserrat in 1677-1678. [TNA]

ADAMS, JOHN, a soldier of the 27th [Inniskilling] Regiment, at Fort George, New York, on 4 September 1757. [NRS.GD45.2.35.2]

ADDISON, NICHOLAS, a Captain of the 52nd [Oxfordshire] Regiment in Boston, New England, a will, 1776. [PWI]

ADYE, STEPHEN P., of the 18th [Royal Regiment of Ireland] Foot, at Charleston Heights, Massachusetts, in 1775. [TNA. WO12.3501]

ALDCROFT, JAMES, Ensign or Volunteer of the 18th [Royal Irish] Regiment around 1770. [PEF.182]; Lieutenant James Aldcroft was promoted to be a Captain in place of Benjamin Chapman on 26 January 1782. [SM.44.55]

ALEXANDER, JOHN, emigrated from Ireland to America in 1773, settled in Ninety-six District, South Carolina, by 1775, a Loyalist soldier who was killed at Kettle Creek. [UEL.I.170]

ALEXANDER, ROBERT, son of John Alexander, emigrated from Ireland to America in 1773, settled in Ninety-six District, South Carolina, by 1775, a Loyalist soldier from 1778 until 1783. [UEL.I.169]

ALLAN, JOHN, a soldier of Lord Blakeney's Regiment, deserted in New York in 1758. [NRS.GD45.2.3.16]

ALLAN, JOHN, a soldier of the 18th [Royal Regiment of Ireland] Foot, in Philadelphia, Pennsylvania, in 1767. [TNA.WO.76/25]

ALPIN, JAMES, from Ireland, a former Sergeant of the 10th [North Lincoln] Regiment, settled in Bathurst, Ontario, on 2 October 1817. [PAO.ms154]

AMBROSE, WILLIAM, a soldier of the 18th [Royal Regiment of Ireland] Foot in Charlestown Heights, Massachusetts, in 1775. [TNA.WO.12.3501]

ANDERSON, GEORGE, born 1764, emigrated from Ireland to America around 1768, settled on Reedy Branch, Ninety-six District, South Carolina, a Loyalist soldier, settled on Bell Isle Bay, Nova Scotia, by 1787. [UEL.II.714]

ANDERSON, JAMES, a soldier of the 18th [Royal Regiment of Ireland] Foot in Charlestown Heights, Massachusetts, in 1775. [TNA.WO.12.3801]

ANDERSON, JOHN, from Kisby, County Monaghan, late of the 9th [Norfolk] Regiment of Foot, applied to settle in Canada on 17 September 1827. [TNA.CO384.16]

ANGLE, JOHN, a soldier of the 18th [Royal Regiment of Ireland] Foot, in Philadelphia, Pennsylvania, in 1770; in New York in 1775. [TNA.W0.76/25]

ANNESLEY, WILLIAM GROVE, fourth son of General A. G. Annesley in County Cork, a Captain of the 4th [King's Own] Regiment, married Eliza Taylor, in St Michael's, Port Royal Mountains, Jamaica, on 8 March 1866. [GM.ns3/1.737]

ANTROBUS, HUGH, Captain or Captain Lieutenant of the 18th [Royal Regiment of Ireland] Foot around 1770. [PEF.103]

ARABIN, FREDERICK, from Maglove, County Meath, a Captain of the Royal Artillery, was married in Quebec, Canada. On 31 May 1823, [GM.93.367]

ARMSTRONG, HENRY, a Captain of the Royal Irish Artillery, died in the West Indies on 14 August 1798. [IS.XVI]

ARMSTRONG, JAMES, a former private of the 70th [Surrey] Regiment, settled in Bathurst, Ontario, on 2 September 1817. [PAO.ms154]

ARMSTRONG, JOHN, emigrated from Ireland to America in 1755 as a soldier of the 48th [Northampton] Regiment until 1763, settled in New York, a Loyalist who moved to Inniskilling, County Fermanagh. [TNA.AO12.100.40]

ARMSTRONG, SAMUEL, from Magharafelt, Londonderry, late a Sergeant of the 52nd [Oxford] Regiment, applied to settle in Canada on 24 March 1827. [TNA.CO384.16]

ARNOLD, ALEXANDER, in Dungannon, County Tyrone, late of the county Yeomanry, applied to settle in Canada on 17 March 1827. [TNA.CO384.16]

ARTERS, WILLIAM, settled in Ninety-six District, South Carolina, a Loyalist soldier, fought at the Siege of Savannah, Georgia, later joined the Militia of Charleston, S.C. as a Lieutenant, moved to Cookstown, County Tyrone, Ireland by 1784. [TNA.AO12.47.154]

ATKINSON, JOHN, born 1775, in Myshall, County Carlow, late of the 20th [East Devon] Regiment of Foot, applied to settle in Canada on 27 July 1827. [TNA.CO384.16]

ATKINSON, Second Lieutenant THOMAS, of the Royal Irish Artillery, was promoted to be Captain in place of Lieutenant Colonel Robert Kingston, on 10 April 1780. [SM.42.391]

ATKINSON, WILLIAM, a soldier of the 18th [Royal Regiment of Ireland] Foot in Philadelphia, Pennsylvania, in 1767. [TNA.WO.76/25]

BAGOTT, CHARLES HERBERT, a Lieutenant of the 32nd [Cornwall] Regiment of Foot, an engineer on St Vincent, died there in 1765. [FDJ.4004]

BAKER, AARON, was appointed as Chaplain of the 27th [Inniskilling] Regiment of Foot on 22 July 1777 in place of Edward Bromhead. [SM.39.391]

BALL, JOHN, born 1680, a Captain of Churchill's Royal Regiment of Dragoons, died in Dublin, Ireland, on 8 March 1755. [SM.17.160]

BALLANTYNE, DAVID, of 37 Cuffe Street, Dublin, an officer of the Templehouse Yeomanry, applied to settle in Canada on 12 April 1827. [TNA.CO384.16]

BANKS, THOMAS, Captain of the Dillon Regiment, of the Irish Brigade in French Service, in America between 1778 and 1783. [IS.XIII.51]

BARBER, JAMES, born in Magharisfelt, Londonderry, served in the 17th [the Loyal Irish] Foot, later in the Royal Hospital Kilmainham. [TNA.WO119.25.249]

BARBER, JAMES, settled in Pennsylvania, later in South Carolina, was Quartermaster of the Camden Regiment of Royal Militia, during the American Revolution, sailed from Charleston, S.C. to Ireland, then settled in Ballymena, County Antrim, by 1783. [TNA.AO12.46.82]

BARKER, WILLIAM, a Second Lieutenant of the Walsh Regiment, of the Irish Brigade in French Service, in America between 1778 and 1783. [IS.XIII.51]

BARRETT, JOHN, born 1734 in Ireland, enlisted in Captain Christopher Gist's Company in Frederick, Virginia, on 15 March 1756. [VCS]

BARRINGTON, JOHN, in Enniscarthy, County Wexford, served for 7 years in the 52nd [Oxfordshire] Regiment of Foot, applied to settle in Canada on 5 March 1827. [TNA.CO384.16]

BARRY, DAVID, a Second Lieutenant of the Walsh Regiment, of the Irish Brigade in French Service, in America between 1778 and 1783. [IS.XIII.51]

BARRY, JAMES, a militiaman in Captain Timothy Thornhill's Company in Barbados in 1679. [H2.80]

BARRY, JOHN, from County Wexford, a merchant shipmaster before 1776, was appointed Captain of USS Lexington in 1776, becoming the father of the American Navy, during the Revolutionary War he captured HMS Edward in 1776, fought at the Battles of Trenton in 1776 and Princeton in 1777 as an artillery officer, was master of the USS Alliance in 1781, he died in Philadelphia on 13 September 1803.

BARRY, Lieutenant RICHARD, in Montserrat in 1677-1678. [TNA]

BARRY, RICHARD, a Lieutenant of the Walsh Regiment, of the Irish Brigade in French Service, in America between 1778 and 1783. [IS.XIII.51]

BARTON, JOHN, in Kildress, County Tyrone, late of Benburb Yeomanry Infantry, applied to settle in Canada on 10 February 1827. [TNA.CO384.16]

BATT, THOMAS, Ensign later Captain or Captain Lieutenant of the 18th [Royal Regiment of Ireland] Foot around 1770, settled in Philadelphia, Pennsylvania, as a wine merchant, a Loyalist in 1776, Major of the 60th [Royal American Fencibles] Regiment, commander of Fort Cumberland in Nova Scotia, where he died in July 1781. [TNA.AO12.106.89][PEF.15/104]

BAYNE, VINCENT, a soldier of the 27th [Inniskilling] Regiment, at Fort George, New York, on 4 September 1757. [NRS.GD45.2.35.2]

BELL, JAMES, a soldier of Lord Blakeney's Regiment, deserted in New York in 1758. [NRS.GD45.2.3.16]

BELL, JOHN, a weaver from County Antrim, Ireland, enlisted in the 58th [Rutlandshire] Regiment in 1767, fought at the Siege of Louisbourg in 1758, the Siege of Quebec in 1759, at Havanna, Cuba, was captured by the French, later rejoined the 58th Regiment in Ireland, in 1768 he volunteered for the 65th [2nd Yorkshire] Regiment bound for Boston, Massachusetts, later in Halifax, Nova Scotia. [NRS.GD45.3.345.85-88]

BELL, MARTIN, a Sergeant of the 18th [Royal Regiment of Ireland] Foot in Philadelphia, Pennsylvania, in 1767; at Charleston Heights, Massachusetts, in 1775. [TNA.WO.76/25; WO.12.3501]

BELL, THOMAS, in Irvinestown, County Fermanagh, for 20 years in the 4th [King's Own] Regiment of Foot, applied to settle in Canada on 9 May 1827. [TNA.CO384.16]

BELLEW, LAURENCE, a Captain of the Walsh Regiment, of the Irish Brigade in French Service, in America between 1778 and 1783. [IS.XIII.51]

BENNETT, EDWARD, a Corporal of the Glengarry Fencibles, settled in Drummond, Ontario, on 16 July 1816. [PAO.ms154]

BENSON, STAWELL, an officer of the Royal Irish Artillery, died in the West Indies on 25 March 1801. [IS.XVI]

BERNARD, GEORGE, was appointed a Captain of the 6th [Inniskilling] Dragoons on 1 July 1774. [London Gazette :5.7.1774]

BETTESWORTH, Colonel, of the Royal Irish Artillery, died in Dublin on 2 February 1790. [SM.52.102]

BEWES, GEORGE, Lieutenant of the 18th [Royal Regiment of Ireland] Foot at Charleston Heights, Massachusetts, in 1775. [TNA.WO12.3501] [PEF.144]; was promoted to Captain of the 18th [Royal Regiment of Ireland] Foot on 22 July 1777 in place of Hugh Lord. [SM.39.391]

BINGHAM, CHARLES, a Captain of the Volunteers of Ireland, a warrant dated New York on 28 December 1782. [HMC.American.iii.289]

BIRCH, Lieutenant JOHN, of the 27th [Inniskilling] Regiment, was appointed Captain of the said regiment on 7 April 1777. [SM.40.223]

BLACK, DAVID, a soldier of the 18th [Royal Regiment of Ireland] Foot in Philadelphia, Pennsylvania, in 1767; at Charleston Heights, Massachusetts, died on 23 August 1775. [TNA.WO.76/25; WO12.3501]

BLACKWOOD, WILLIAM, Captain or Captain Lieutenant of the 18th [Royal Regiment of Ireland] Foot around 1770. [PEF.108]

BLOOMER, JOHN, formerly a soldier of the 104th [North British Fusiliers] Regiment, settled in Drummond, Ontario, on 22 August 1816. [PAO.ms154]

BLAKELY, CHAMBERS, emigrated from Ireland to America, settled in Ninety-six District, South Carolina, a Loyalist militiaman. [UEL.I.676]

BLAKENEY, Sir W. L., was appointed Colonel of the 27th [Inniskilling] Regiment on 22 June 1737, later, as Lord Blakeney he was at Fort George, New York, on 4 September 1757. [NRS.GD45.2.35.2][IR.153]

BLAIR, THOMAS, a soldier of the 18th [Royal Regiment of Ireland] Foot in Philadelphia, Pennsylvania, in 1770, was transferred in New York on 9 October 1774. [TNA.W0.76/25]

BLAKENEY, THOMAS, born in northern Ireland, settled at Fort Lime, English Neighbourhood, New Jersey, a Loyalist who joined the British Army, was impressed into the Royal Navy from 1777 to 1783, settled in England. [TNA.AO12.14.254]

BLAKENEY, WILLIAM, born in Ireland on 7 September 1672, Lieutenant General of the 18th [Royal Regiment of Ireland] Foot, fought at the Siege of Cartagena, Cuba, in 1741 and possibly in North America during the French and Indian War, in Fort George, New York, in September 1757; died in Limerick on 20 September 1761. [SM.23.558][NRS.GD45.2.35.2]

BRANING, THOMAS, born 1727 in Ireland, a tailor in Fredericksburg, Virginia, a soldier of Captain Robert Spotswood's Company in Fort Young, Virginia, on 4 October 1757. [VCS]

BLUNDELL, DIXIE, an officer of the Royal Irish Artillery, died in the West Indies on 23 July 1796. [IS.XVI]

BREADY, LUKE, emigrated from Ireland to America in 1763, settled at Crown Point, New York, until 1776, a Loyalist sailor and engineer in Canada, settled in New Johnstown, Ontario, by 1788. [UEL.I.405]

BLEAKNEY, DAVID, emigrated from Ireland to America in 1767, settled in Ninety-six District, South Carolina, by 1776, a Loyalist soldier during the American War, later settled at Petty Coat Jack, Westmoreland, Nova Scotia. [UEL.I.259]

BLOOMER, JOHN, a former soldier of the 104th [New Brunswick Fencibles] Regiment, settled in Drummond, Ontario, on 22 August 1816. [PAO.ms154]

BOLTON, JOHN, a soldier of the 18th [Royal Regiment of Ireland] Foot in Philadelphia, Pennsylvania, in 1767. [TNA.WO.76/25]

BOSWELL, JAMES, born 1708 in Ireland, a weaver who enlisted in Captain Thomas Cocke's Company in Stafford, Virginia, on 24 September 1755. [VCS]

BOVILL, THOMAS, in Grange, County Antrim, a former Corporal of the Royal Regiment of Artillery, applied to settle in Prescott, Upper Canada, on 1 March 1827, possible emigrated via Belfast to Quebec on 25 April 1827. [TNA.CO384.16]

BOWMAN, JAMES, born in Ireland, a surgeon major of the British forces in Quebec in 1760s, died there in 1787. [DCB]

BOYLE, JOHN, a soldier of the 18th [Royal Regiment of Ireland] Foot in Philadelphia, Pennsylvania, in 1767, at Charleston Heights, Massachusetts, in 1775. [TNA.WO.76/25; WO12.3501]

BOYLE, ..., an Ensign, formerly a Lieutenant of the 1st Battalion of Brigadier De Lancey's Brigade, emigrated to America in 1777, fought at the Sieges of Savannah and York, and with Colonel Ferguson at King's Mountain, a memorial dated 13 February 1783. [HMC.American.iii.356]

BRADLEY, PATRICK, a soldier of the 18th [Royal Regiment of Ireland] Foot, at Charleston Heights, Massachusetts, in 1775. [TNA.WO12.3501]

BRADLEY, THOMAS, in Portadown, for 7 years a soldier of the 81st [Lincolnshire] Foot, applied to settled in Canada on 23 March 1827. [TNA.CO384.16]

BRADSHAW, JAMES, born in Ireland, settled in Kingbury, Charlotte County, New York, Captain of Loyalist Militia in 1777, moved to the Bay of Quinty, Canada. [UEL.II.1204]

BRANCELIN, CHARLES, Quartermaster of the Walsh Regiment, of the Irish Brigade in French Service, in America between 1778 and 1783. [IS.XIII.51]

BRANING, THOMAS, born 1727 in Ireland, a tailor in Fredericksburg, Virginia, a soldier in Captain Robert Spotswood's Company at Fort Young in 1757.

BRANNAN, PATRICK, of General John Sebright's Company of the 18th [Royal Regiment of Ireland] Foot, was executed at Fort Pitt, Ohio, in 17..

BRIANT, JOHN, born 1729 in Ireland, a clothier who enlisted in Captain William Bronaugh's Company, in Fairfax, Virginia, in October 1755. [VCS]

BRIGHT, JAMES, a former Sergeant of the Glengarry Fencibles, settled in Bastrad, Ontario, on 20 October 1819. [PAO.ms154]

BRIGHT, THOMAS, a former Sergeant of the Glengarry Fencibles, settled in Drummond, Ontario, on 16 July 1816. [PAO.ms154]

BRISBAND, JOHN, emigrated from Ireland to America about 1770, settled in Saratoga, New York, joined the British Army in

1777, served in Colonel Jessup's Regiment of Loyal Rangers, and later in Colonel Delancy's as a Sergeant, moved to Canada and settled at Fanning's Borough, Ontario, by 1786. [PAO.LC.630][UEL.II.768]

BRISBANE, ROBERT, emigrated from Ireland to America, settled in Saratoga, New York, a Loyalist soldier, at Messessquibui Bay, Canada, by 1788. [OBA]

BRISON, JOHN, emigrated from Ireland to Carolina in 1772, settled in Ninety-six District, S.C., a Loyalist and British soldier from 1780, settled in Rawdon, Nova Scotia, by 1786. [UEL.I.176]

BROBSON, JOSEPH, emigrated from Ireland to Philadelphia, Pennsylvania, around 1762, joined the Royal Militia of South Carolina and served with the Engineers Department, was captured in Charleston, South Carolina, in 1781, settled in Moneymore, Ireland, by 1789. [TNA.SC12.43.298]

BROGAN, JOHN, late of the Prince of York's Chasseurs, settled in Bathurst, Ontario, on 7 October 1819. [PAO.ms154]

BROWNE, HENRY, a Lieutenant of the 22ND [Cheshire] Regiment [Louisbourg Grenadiers], son of John Browne in Westport, Castlebarr, Ireland, fought at Louisbourg, Acadia, a letter dated 17 November 1759. [NAM.ms7808-93-2][NLI.18444] [TNA.WO.17.124]

BROWN, JAMES, a carpenter in Southwark, Philadelphia, joined the Army in Philadelphia, Pennsylvania, served as a guide, settled in Mannybrannon, Coleraine, Londonderry, Ireland, by 1784. [TNA.13.90.204-206]

BROWN, JOHN, born 1729 in Ireland, a clothier who enlisted in Captain William Bronaugh's Company, in Stafford, Virginia, in November 1755. [VCS]

BROWNE, JOHN, Lieutenant of the Dillon Regiment, of the Irish Brigade in French Service, in America between 1778 and 1783. [IS.XIII.51]

BROWN, NEILL, born 1724, from County Antrim, settled in Fog's Manor, Chester County, Pennsylvania, about 1766, fought as a Loyalist with the British Army at Lexington, Massachusetts, in

1775, returned to Ireland and settled near Belfast by 1788. [TNA.AO12.102.135]

BROWN, ROBERT, a soldier of the 18th [Royal Regiment of Ireland] Foot in Charlestown Heights, Massachusetts, died on 2 July 1775. [TNA.WO.12.3801]

BROWNE, THOMAS, Second Lieutenant of the Dillon Regiment, of the Irish Brigade in French Service, in America between 1778 and 1783. [IS.XIII.51]

BROWN, WILLIAM, a Captain of the 3rd [Kent] Regiment in Boston, New England, a will in 1776. [PWI]

BRUERE, GEORGE, Lieutenant of the 18th [Royal Regiment of Ireland] Foot, at Charleston Heights, Massachusetts, in 1775. [TNA.WO12.3501][PEF.146]

BRUIN, ROBERT, in Kilria, late of the 2nd Battalion of the Royal Artillery, applied to settle in Canada on 9 May 1827. [TNA.CO384.16]

BRUN, Captain WILLIAM, an Irishman, led 130 Irish Catholics from St Kitts to Para on the Amazon River in Brazil in August 1646. [HS.2nd series, 171/122]

BRUNNAN, CHRISTOPHER, a soldier of the 2nd Battalion of the 84th [Royal Highland Emigrants] Regiment, aboard the frigate Raleigh bound from New York to Charleston, South Carolina, in 1780. [NRS.GD174.2405]

BRUNNAN, PETER, a soldier of the 2nd Battalion of the 84th [Royal Highland Emigrants] Regiment of Foot, aboard the frigate Raleigh bound from New York to Charleston, South Carolina, in 1780. [NRS.GD174.2405]

BRUSH, CREAN, probably from Ireland, settled in Vermont, a Loyalist, died in 1778, probate 14 April 1778, New York City. [TNA.AO.12.30.212]

BRYAN, JOHN, from Ireland, a former private of the 51st [King's Own] Regiment of Foot, settled in Drummond, Ontario, on 4 October 1817. [PAO.ms154]

BRYANT, JOHN, born 1728 in Ireland, a planter in Fairfax, Virginia, a soldier of Captain Henry Woodward's Company in Virginia, on 11 September 1757. [VCS]

BRYSON, ANDREW, from Bangor, County Down, a United Irishman, who was transported to the West Indies, for enforced military service, a soldier on St Pierre, later in New York, an account dated 1801. [PRONI.T1373]

BUCHANAN, WILLIAM, II, an officer of the Royal Irish Artillery, died in the West Indies on 12 February 1797. [IS.XVI]

BUCKELLY, THOMAS, a pedlar from Wexford, later a soldier of the 58th [Rutlandshire] Regiment of Foot, was found guilty of robbing an officer's quarters in Quebec and was sentenced to 1000 lashes. [TNA.WO71.46.10-14; WO25.435.67]

BUCKLEY, HUGH, in Lisburn, having served for five years in the 2nd [Queen's Own] Regiment of Foot, applied to settle in Canada on 27 March 1827. [TNA.CO384.16]

BUCKLEY, JOHN, a soldier of Lord Blakeney's Regiment, deserted in New York in 1758. [NRS.GD45.2.3.16]

BUCKLEY, MICHAEL, late a private of the Glengarry Fencibles, settled in Drummond, Ontario, on 16 July 1816. [PAO.ms154]

BUFFIN, JOHN, a soldier of the 18th [Royal Regiment of Ireland] Foot, a prisoner in New York in 1775. [TNA.WO.76/25]

BULGER, THOMAS, a soldier of the 18th [Royal Regiment of Ireland] Foot in Philadelphia, Pennsylvania, in 1772. [TNA.WO.76/25]

BURKE, AEDANUS, born 1743 in County Galway, settled in Charleston, South Carolina, in 1775, a Revolutionary officer in South Carolina, died in 1802. [Hibernian Society of South Carolina]

BURKE, DENIS, born 1752 in Ireland, a M.D., late assistant surgeon at West Point, New York, died in Washington, D.C., on 29 June 1852. [GM ns 38.433]

BURKE, Dr REDMUND, from Ireland to America, a surgeon's mate, later Surgeon Major in the Southern Department, returned to Ireland by 1783. [TNA.AO12.46.1]

BURKE, MICHAEL, born 1780, late of the 6th [Inniskilling Dragoons] Regiment, applied to settle in Canada on 12 June 1827. [TNA.CO384.16]

BURK, PATRICK, late of the Royal Sappers, settled in Lanark, Ontario, on 1 November 1820. [PAO.ms154]

BURKE, RICHARD, a militiaman in Captain John Sampson's Company on Barbados in 1679. [H2.79]

BURKE, TOBY, a militiaman in Colonel Christopher's Regiment in Barbados in 1679. [TNA.CO1.44.47]

BURKE, WILLIAM, a soldier in Placentia, Newfoundland, in 1732. [TNA.CO194.24.109]

BURNE, DENIS, a militiaman in Captain Tim Thornhill's company in Barbados in 1679. [TNA.CO1.44.47] [H2.80]

BURNS, JAMES, a soldier of the 18th [Royal Regiment of Ireland] Foot at Charleston Heights, Massachusetts, in 1775. [TNA.WO12.3501]

BURNS, JAMES, in Dunmanway, late of the 25th [King's Own Scottish Borderers] Regiment of Foot, applied to settle in Canada on 8 February 1827. [TNA.CO384.16]

BURNS, JOHN, born 1729 in Ireland, a collier who was recruited into Stewart's Light Horse in Virginia on 4 December 1755. [VCS]

BURNS, JOHN, a soldier of the 2nd Battalion of the 84th [Royal Highland Emigrants] Regiment, aboard the frigate Raleigh bound from New York to Charleston, South Carolina, in 1780. [NRS.GD174.2405]

BURNS, MICHAEL, born 1722 in Ireland, a planter in Lunenburg, Virginia, a soldier in Major Andrew Lewis's Company in Virginia in 1757.

BURNS, THOMAS, settled in Lower Providence, Chester County, Pennsylvania, as a farmer, joined the British Army in 1777, returned to Killileagh, County Down, by 1789. [TNA.AO12.43.322]

BURNS, THOMAS, from Ireland, a former private of the 4th [Royal Veteran] Battalion, settled in Burgess, Ontario, on 30 June 1817. [PAO.ms154]

BURRELL, JOHN, in Moy, Loughgall parish, County Armagh, late of the militia, applied to settle in Canada on 13 April 1827. [TNA.CO384.16]

BURROWS, ROBERT, in Magherafelt, County Londonderry, late of the 73rd [Perthshire] Regiment of Foot, applied to settle in Canada on 1 March 1827. [TNA.CO384.16]

BURROWS, WILLIAM, from Ireland, formerly a private of the 77th [Montgomery's Highlanders] Regiment, settled in Ontario in September 1822. [PAO.ms154]

BUSBY, THOMAS, born in Ireland, enlisted in the 27th [Inniskilling] Regiment of Foot in Cork, sent to Halifax, Nova Scotia, in 1757, fought at Ticonderoga, and at Carillon and Fort Saint Frederic, also at Grenada, Martinique and Havana, was discharged in Quebec in 1767, from 1768 until 1796 he was barrack-master in Montreal, he died there on 22 October 1798. [DCB]

BUTLER, HUMPHREY, a soldier of Captain Liston's Company in Barbados in 1679. [TNA.CO1.44.47]

BUTLER, PATRICK, in Roscrea, late of the 25th [King's Own Scottish Borderers] Regiment of Foot, applied to settle in Canada on 12 April 1827. [TNA.CO384.16]

BUTLER, Captain THOMAS, on Nevis or St Kitts, probate 1689, PCC. [TNA]

BUTLER, WILLIAM, a soldier in Colonel Thornhill's Company in Barbados in 1679. [TNA.CO1.44.47.191-196]

BUTTRICKE, GEORGE, Staff Officer of the 18th [Royal Irish Regiment] Foot, quartermaster in Illinois in 1768, quartermaster of the 18th [Royal Regiment of Ireland] Foot in 1770; in Boston, New England, in 1775. [TNA.WO.76/25][PEF.20/201]

BUTTRICKE, GEORGE, an Ensign of the 18th [Royal Regiment of Ireland] Foot, was promoted to Lieutenant of the 18th Regiment on 10 December 1776. [SM.38.677]

BYGRAVE, WILLIAM, late of the Prince of York's Chasseurs, settled in Bathurst, Ontario, on 7 October 1819. [PAO.ms154]

BYRNES, JOHN, in Ballymalion, County Longford, formerly a Sergeant of the 38th [Stafford] Foot, applied to settle in Canada on 6 April 1827. [TNACO384.16]

CAGHLAN, WILLIAM, a soldier of Captain Samuel Woodward's Company of Militia in Barbados on 8 January 1679. [H2.156]

CAHILL, MICHAEL, from Ireland, a former private of the 19th Dragoons, settled in Drummond, Ontario, on 22 August 1817. [PAO.ms154]

CAHILL, MICHAEL, in Kilmainham Royal Hospital, served for 18 years in the 16th Lancers, applied to settle in Canada on 15 August 1827. [TNA.CO384.16]

CAHILL, THOMAS, from Ireland, a former private of the Glengarry Fencibles, settled in Bathurst, Ontario, on 6 November 1816. [PAO.ms154]

CALDWELL, HENRY, born 1738 in Ireland, son of Sir John Caldwell the High Sheriff of Fermanagh, a Colonel of the British Army during the Seven Years War, 1756-1763, he fought at Louisbourg, and Quebec, Governor of Fort Augusta in the West Indies, later the Receiver General of Quebec, died in 1810. [DCB]

CALLAGHAR, P., a Corporal of the 51st [King's Own] Regiment, died in the Barbados in 182-. [St Michael's Cathedral tablet, Bridgetown, Barbados]

CALLAHAN, CHARLES, emigrated from Ireland and settled at Pownalburg, Maine, he was appointed master of the armed sloop General Gage which was wrecked and he drowned of the coast of Nova Scotia in 1777. [PAO.LC.612]

CALLAGHAN, DENIS, a militiaman in Barbados in 1679. [TNA.CO1.44.47]

CALLENANE, DERBY, a militiaman of Captain Samuel Woodward's Company in Barbados in 1679. [TNA.CO1.44.47] [H2.156]

CAMPBELL, ALEXANDER, possibly from Cork, a merchant in Boston, Massachusetts, before 1776, fought at Bunker's Hill in General Robert Pigot's Brigade, a Captain of the 84th [Royal Highland Emigrants] Regiment, as Major of the Royal South American Rangers died at Black River, Jamaica. [TNA.AO.12.50.101]

CAMPBELL, DANIEL, born in Ireland on 19 September 1730, a militiaman of Albany County, New York around 1780, died on 16 August 1802. [ANY.I.73]

CAMPBELL, JAMES, a soldier of the 18th [Royal Regiment of Ireland], Foot, deserted in Philadelphia, Pennsylvania, on 11 June 1772. [TNA.WO.76/25]

CAMPBELL, ROBERT, a soldier of the 18th [Royal Regiment of Ireland] Foot in Philadelphia, Pennsylvania, in 1770, transferred on 25 October 1770. [TNA.WO.76/25]

CANAVAN, Sergeant WILLIAM, on Montserrat in 1677-1678. [TNA]

CARDEN, Lieutenant, of the 60th [Royal American] Regiment, Captain of Artillery and Engineer on the expedition, referred to in a long letter from St Fernando de Omao, on the Mosquito Shore, Honduras, dated 21 October 1779. [SM.41.666-673]

CARLETON, GUY, born 3 September 1724 in Strabane, County Tyrone, an officer of the 25th [King's Own Scottish Borderers] Regiment of Foot, fought in the French and Indian War, notably at Louisbourg, 1758, and at the Siege of Quebec in 1759, Governor of Quebec from 1768 until 1778, led the defence of Quebec in 1775, died in England on 10 November 1808.

CARLEY, PATRICK, in Monaghan, served 9 years in the 49th [Hertfordshire] Regiment and the 29th [Worcester] Foot, applied to settle in Canada on 10 March 1827. [TNA.CO384.16]

CARNES, JOHN, a soldier of the 18th [Royal Regiment of Ireland] Foot, in Charlestown Heights, Massachusetts, in 1775. [TNA.WO.12.3501]

CARRIGAN, PATRICK, settled in Saratoga, New York, a Loyalist soldier from 1776 to 1777, returned to Ireland in 1778. [TNA.AO12.26.424]

CARROL, JOHN, born 1733 in Ireland, a sailor in Augusta, Virginia, enlisted in November 1756, a soldier of Colonel George Washington's Company in August 1757. [VCS]

CARROLL, JOHN, born 1731 in Ireland, a waterman in Norfolk County, Virginia, enlisted in the Virginia Regiment on 19 May 1756. [VCS]

CARROLL, MICHAEL, a soldier of Colonel Thornhill's Company in Barbados in 1679. [TNA.CO1.44.47]

CARSCALLEN, EDWARD, was born in Ireland, settled at Camden District, Charlotte County, New York, a Loyalist officer during the war, moved to Canada by 1783. [OBA.907] [UEL.II.1023]

CARSON, CHRISTOPHER, a soldier of Lord Blakeney's Regiment, deserted in New York in 1758. [NRS.GD45.2.3.16]

CARSON, JAMES, late of the Prince of York's Chasseurs, settled in Beckwith, Ontario, on 22 September 1819. [PAO.ms154]

CARWIG, JOHN, born 1713 in Ireland, a shoemaker who enlisted in Captain Thomas Cocke's Company in Northumberland, Virginia, on 7 January 1756. [VCS]

CASEY, Lieutenant DAVID O'BRIAN, of the Royal Navy, an account of a mutiny aboard HMS Hermoine in the Caribbean in September 1797. [NMM]

CASSIDY, JOHN, at Shannon Bridge, late of the 12th Veteran Battalion, applied to settle in Canada in April 1827. [TNA.CO384.16]

CATER, JOHN, a Sergeant of the 18th [Royal Regiment of Ireland] Foot in Charlestown Heights, Massachusetts, in 1775. [TNA.WO.12.3801]

CATHCART, ALEXANDER and JOSHUA, serving in Canada from 1759-1760. [PRONI. Perceval pp.D906]

CAVAN, BRIAN, a militiaman in Captain John Sampson's Company on Barbados in 1679. [H2.79]

CAVANAGH, MICHAEL, formerly a Sergeant of the 70th [Surrey] Regiment, settled in Bathurst, Ontario, on 10 July 1820. [PAO.ms154]

CHAMBEY, RICHARD, in Granard, County Longford, late of the 60th [Royal American Regiment] of Foot, applied to settle in Canada on 20 March 1827. [TNA.CO384.16]

CHAMBRE, WILLIAM, journal of his service with the 11th [North Devon] Regiment in Canada between 1838 and 1840. PRO.I.M7035.22]

CHANDLER, Captain Lieutenant EDWARD, of the 49th [Hertfordshire] Foot, was promoted to be Captain of the 27th [Inniskilling] Foot on 1 April 1780. [SM.42.335]

CHAPMAN, BENJAMIN, Captain or Captain Lieutenant of the 18th [Royal Regiment of Ireland] Foot, around 1770. [PEF.110]

CHAPPELL, Captain, from Ireland, was taken hostage on St Kitts by the Spanish in 1631. [HS, 2nd series, 56.13]

CHESNEY, ALEXANDER, born 1755, emigrated from Ireland to America around 1768, settled in South Carolina, formerly a Captain of Militia in South Carolina before the American Revolution, settled as a Customs Officer in Belfast, Ireland, an affidavit, 1783; letter from Prospect, Kilkeel, County Down, re the behaviour of the people of Charleston, S.C., during the War of Independence; a journal from 1755 to 1815]. [TNA.AO.13.125.366-388] [PRONI.T1095] [ISPO. Rebellion pp1796]

CHOW, JOHN, a soldier of the 18th [Royal Regiment of Ireland] Foot in Philadelphia, Pennsylvania, in 1767. [TNA.WO.76/25]

CHRISTIE, GABRIEL, born 16 September 1722 son of James Christie, a merchant in Stirling, and his wife Catherine Napier, was a Lieutenant of the 27th [Inniskilling] Foot, fought the Jacobites at Culloden in 1745, by 1756 he was Captain of the 44th Foot in Canada, and Quartermaster General in North America, he fought at Quebec in 1758, in 1767 he was granted land on Prince Edward Island, in 1775 he was Lieutenant Colonel of the 60th [Royal American] Foot in Montreal, [letter 12.9.1776], later he was Lieutenant Colonel of the Royal Rifles Regiment in the West Indies, in 1798 he was appointed Commander in Chief in Canada, he died in Quebec on 26 January 1799. [DCB] [JAHR.26.136] [JCTP.74.401]

CHURCHILL, SAMUEL, late of the Sappers and Miners, settled in Burgess, Ontario, on 18 September 1819. [PAO.ms154]

CLANSEY, CORNELIUS, a militiaman of Colonel Christopher Lyne's Regiment in Barbados in 1679. [TNA.CO1.44.47]

CLANCY, THOMAS, a soldier of the New York Militia in 1687. [NYSA]

CLARK, JOHN, formerly a private of the Canadian Fencibles, settled in Burgess, Ontario, on 30 September 1816. [PAO.ms154]

CLARK, JOHN, in Tipperary, late Quartermaster of the 99th [Lanarkshire] Regiment, applied to settle in Canada on 7 February 1827. [TNA.CO384.16]

CLERK, JOHN, in Tipperary, a former officer of the 99th [Lanarkshire] Regiment, applied to settled in Canada on 21 March 1827. [TNA.CO384.16]

CLARK, ROBERT, late of the Prince of York's Chasseurs, settled in Bathurst, Ontario, on 7 October 1819. [PAO.ms154]

CLERK, MATTHEW, an engineer of Lord Blakeney's Regiment, was killed at the Siege of Ticonderoga, New York, in July 1758. [NRS.GD18.4201.3.4]; letters from New York in 1757-1758. [NRS.GD18.4201/3/4]

CLARKE, WILLIAM, a former Sergeant of the Carlow Militia, settled in Drummond, Ontario, on 12 August 1817, moved to Montague, Ontario, on 30 November 1817. [PAO.ms154]

CLOSSY, Dr SAMUEL, was educated at Dublin University, emigrated to America in 1763, a surgeon's mate at the Military Hospital in New York from 1776 to 1780, a Loyalist who was buried in St Andrew's Church, Dublin, on 24 August 1786. [TNA.AO12.19.216]

COGHLAN, TERENCE, Second Captain of the Dillon Regiment, of the Irish Brigade in French Service, in America between 1778 and 1783. [IS.XIII.51]

COLEMAN, DANIEL, late of the Royal Sappers, settled in Lanark, Ontario, on 1 November 1820. [PAO.ms154]

COLLINS, DAVID, born 1734 in Ireland, a sailor, enlisted in Captain David Bell's Company, in Virginia on 1 September 1755. [VCS]

COLLINS, EDWARD, a soldier of Captain Harrison's Company in Barbados in 1679. [TNA.CO1.44.47]

COLLINS, THOMAS, Captain of His Majesty's 11th West Indies Regiment, a will, 1802. [PWI]

CLARK, JOHN, formerly a private of the Canadian Fencibles, settled in Burgess, Ontario, on 30 September 1816. [PAO.ms154]

CLARK, JOHN, in Tipperary, late Quartermaster of the 99th [Lanarkshire] Regiment, applied to settle in Canada on 7 February 1827. [TNA.CO384.16]

CLERK, JOHN, in Tipperary, a former officer of the 99th [Lanarkshire] Regiment, applied to settled in Canada on 21 March 1827. [TNA.CO384.16]

CLARK, ROBERT, late of the Prince of York's Chasseurs, settled in Bathurst, Ontario, on 7 October 1819. [PAO.ms154]

CLERK, MATTHEW, an engineer of Lord Blakeney's Regiment, was killed at the Siege of Ticonderoga, New York, in July 1758. [NRS.GD18.4201.3.4]; letters from New York in 1757-1758. [NRS.GD18.4201/3/4]

CLARKE, WILLIAM, a former Sergeant of the Carlow Militia, settled in Drummond, Ontario, on 12 August 1817, moved to Montague, Ontario, on 30 November 1817. [PAO.ms154]

CLOSSY, Dr SAMUEL, was educated at Dublin University, emigrated to America in 1763, a surgeon's mate at the Military Hospital in New York from 1776 to 1780, a Loyalist who was buried in St Andrew's Church, Dublin, on 24 August 1786. [TNA.AO12.19.216]

COGHLAN, TERENCE, Second Captain of the Dillon Regiment, of the Irish Brigade in French Service, in America between 1778 and 1783. [IS.XIII.51]

COLEMAN, DANIEL, late of the Royal Sappers, settled in Lanark, Ontario, on 1 November 1820. [PAO.ms154]

COLLINS, DAVID, born 1734 in Ireland, a sailor, enlisted in Captain David Bell's Company, in Virginia on 1 September 1755. [VCS]

COLLINS, EDWARD, a soldier of Captain Harrison's Company in Barbados in 1679. [TNA.CO1.44.47]

COLLINS, THOMAS, Captain of His Majesty's 11th West Indies Regiment, a will, 1802. [PWI]

COLVILL, MATHEW, son of Rev. Dr Alexander Colvill and his wife Jane in Dromore, Ireland, settled in Bladen County, North Carolina, a Colonel of a Loyalist Provincial Regiment during the rebellion, who was murdered there, [TNA.AO.12.37.117]

CONCANNON, ..., a midshipman of the Royal Navy, referred to in a long letter from St Fernando de Omao, on the Mosquito Shore, Honduras, dated 21 October 1779. [SM.41.666-673]

CONDON, RICHARD, a shoemaker from Ireland, deserted from Benjamin Stoddart's Company of Militia, in Annapolis, Maryland, in August 1746. [MG.68]

CONKLIN, GRAHAM, late of the Prince of York's Chasseurs, settled in Bathurst, Ontario, on 21 October 1819. [PAO.ms154]

CONNELL, DARBY, a soldier of the 2nd Battalion of the 84th [Royal Highland Emigrants] Regiment, aboard the frigate Raleigh bound from New York to Charleston, South Carolina, in 1780. [NRS.GD174.2405]

CONNELL, HUGH, emigrated from Ireland to America in 1772, settled in Cherry Valley, New York, a Loyalist soldier in Sir John Johnston's Regiment, [King's Royal Regiment of New York] afterwards settled at the Bay of Quinte, Canada, by 1788. [TNA.AO12.33.169/171]

CONNELL, MORRIS, a soldier of Captain Samuel Woodward's Company of Militia in Barbados on 8 January 1679. [H2.156]

CONNELL, NICOLAS, a militiaman in Captain Thomas Helm's Company on Barbados in 1679. [H2.154]

CONNELL, REDMOND, a soldier of the 2nd Battalion of the 84th [Royal Highland Emigrants] Regiment, aboard the frigate Raleigh bound from New York to Charleston, South Carolina, in 1780. [NRS.GD174.2405]

CONNON, TEIGE, a militiaman of Captain George Lillington's Company in Barbados in 1679. [TNA.CO1.44.47] [H2.51]

CONNOR, JOHN, a soldier of the 2nd Battalion of the 84th [Royal Highland Emigrants] Regiment, aboard the frigate Raleigh bound from New York to Charleston, South Carolina, in 1780. [NRS.GD174.2405]

CONNOR, MARTIN, from Ireland, formerly in the Royal Navy, settled in Drummond, Ontario, on 6 April 1818. [PAO.ms154]

CONNOR, MICHAEL, from Ireland, formerly a private of the Carlow Militia, settled in Oxford, Ontario, on 9 July 1817. [PAO.ms154]

CONNOR, THOMAS, late of the York Chasseurs, settled in Bathurst, Ontario, on 22 September 1819. [PAO.ms154]

CONOLLY, DANIEL, born 17 March 1738 in Oldcastle, Ireland, a soldier who fought at the Siege of Louisbourg, the Siege of Quebec, also at Martinique and Havannah, died in Anstruther, Fife, on 22 March 1818. [SM.81.499]

CONNOLLY, Lieutenant Colonel JOHN, letters, of the Provincial line, 1782, 1783. [HMC.American.ii.485/488; iii.349]; a memorial dated London on 1 March 1783 re Niagara and Detroit. [HMC.American.iii.380]

CONNELLY, WILLIAM, Lieutenant of the 18th [Royal Regiment of Ireland] Foot around 1770. [PEF.149]

CONROY, THOMAS, a soldier of the 18th [Royal Regiment of Ireland] Foot, in New York, in 1775. [TNA.WO.76/25]

CONSTANTINE, MATTHEW, a soldier of the 18th [Royal Regiment of Ireland] Foot in Philadelphia, Pennsylvania, in 1767. [TNA.WO.76/25]

CONWAY, TIMOTHY, born 1715 in Ireland, a shoemaker, enlisted as a soldier of the Second Company of Rangers in Virginia on 21 October 1755. [VCS]

COOKE, JOHN, a soldier of the 18th [Royal Regiment of Ireland] Foot in Philadelphia, Pennsylvania, in 1767. [TNA.WO.76/25]

COOK, Captain THOMAS, in Montserrat in 1682. [NRS.HCAS.AC7/9]

COOK, ..., a Lieutenant of Lord Blakeney's Regiment, was wounded at the Siege of Ticonderoga, New York, in July 1758. [NRS]

COOPER, JOHN, a soldier of the 18th [Royal Regiment of Ireland] Foot in Philadelphia, Pennsylvania, in 1767. [TNA.WO.76/25]

COURTNEY, JOSEPH, from Ireland, late of the 5th Dragoon Guards, settled in Burgess, Ontario, on 15 December 1817. [PAO.ms154]

COTTER, JAMES, emigrated from Ireland to America in 1757, settled in Johnstown, Tryon County, New York, a Loyalist soldier in Sir John Johnston's [King's Royal Regiment of New York] from 1776 until 1783, settled at Couteau de Lac, Canada, by 1787. [TNA.AO228.181/182][OBA.903][UEL.II.1021]

COTTERAL, THOMAS, a soldier of the 27th [Inniskilling] Regiment, at Fort George, New York, on 4 September 1757. [NRS.GD45.2.35.2]

COULSON, JAMES, an officer of the Royal Irish Artillery, died in the West Indies on 22 May 1794. [S.XVI]

COULTER, ANDREW, born in Ireland, a soldier of the 46th [South Devonshire] Regiment in 1757, a farmer at Fort George by 1764, a Loyalist soldier from 1777 until 1783, then settled at Carlisle Bay, Canada, by 1787. [OBA.241]

COYLE, CHARLES, born 1739 in County Tyrone, a soldier of the 43rd [Monmouthshire] Regiment of Foot which fought in the St Lawrence Campaign. [TNA.WO.121.6]

CRAGIE, ANDREW, a soldier of the 18th [Royal Regiment of Ireland] Foot in Philadelphia, Pennsylvania, in 1767. [TNA.WO.76/25]

CRAIG, JOHN, born 1731 in Ireland, a weaver who was recruited into Stewart's Light Horse in Virginia on 4 December 1755. [VCS]

CRAWFORD, GEORGE, Major of the 2nd West Indies Regiment, a will, 1808. [PWI]

CRAWLEY, JOHN, born 1728 in Ireland, a distiller who enlisted in Captain Christopher Gist's Company in Frederick, Virginia, on 2 March 1756. [VCS]

CREOCH, JOHN, born 1732 in Ireland, a bookbinder in Stafford, Virginia, a Sergeant in Captain Thomas Waggener's Company at Fort Holland in August 1757.

CORAN, JOHN, late of the Prince of York's Chasseurs, settled in Bathurst, Ontario, on 7 October 1819. [PAO.ms154]

CORBET, Brigadier JOHN, a petition 'for a moiety of the matters in the hands of the President and Council of Maryland', ca1710. [NLI.Ormonde pp.ms.2382]

CORMACK, JOHN, a planter and Colonel of Militia on Montserrat in 1677. [TNA]

CORMACK, JOHN, an Ensign on Montserrat in 1677-1678. [TNA]

CORNAN, JAMES, formerly a private of the 104th [North British Regiment, Foot, settled in Beckwith, Ontario, on 6 June 1817. [PAO.ms154]

CORREY, EDWARD, born 1740 in Ireland, 5 foot six inches in height, strongly made, grey eyes and brown hair, was recruited in Boston, Massachusetts, by Ensign John Archbold of the 40th [Somerset] Regiment, on 19 January 1758. [NRS.GD45.2.35.9]

CORRY, JAMES, emigrated from Ireland to America in 1756, settled in Albany County, New York, a Loyalist soldier in James Rogers Corps of King's Rangers, died in Lancaster, Canada, after 1782. [TNA.AO12.33.13-15]

COSBY, Sir WILLIAM, born 1690 in Strabally, Queen's County, Ireland, son of Alexander Cosby, he was Colonel of the 18th [Royal Regiment of Ireland] Foot from 1717 until 1732, then governor of New York and New Jersey until his death on 10 March 1736.

COSGROVE, FRANCIS, born in 1768, a shoemaker who enlisted in the British Army in Burr, King's County, Ireland, in 1804, was discharged in St John in 1818, and settled in Dalhousie, Nova Scotia, in 1820. [TNA.WO.25.548]

COTTER, JOHN, born 1720 in Ireland, a planter in enlisted in Captain David Bell's Company in Chesterfield, Virginia, in October 1755. [VCS]

COTTON, Captain WILLIAM, of the 27th [Inniskilling] Foot, was promoted to be Major in place of Nicholas Wade on 1 April 1780. [SM.42.335]

CRESTWICK, JOSEPH, a Corporal of the 18th [Royal Regiment of Ireland] Foot, in Charlestown Heights, Massachusetts, in 1775. [TNA.WO.12.3501]

CROFTON, Sir MALBY, 'he served under the immortal Wolfe at the Siege of Quebec', died in County Sligo on 29 February 1808. [SM.70.239]

CRONY, RICHARD, late Corporal of the York Chasseurs, settled in Drummond, Ontario, on 8 July 1820. [PAO.ms154]

CROSBY, EDWARD, Lieutenant of the 18th [Royal Regiment of Ireland] Foot around 1770. [PEF.152]

CROSBY, JAMES, emigrated from Ireland to America around 1754, settled at Drowning Creek, North Carolina, a militiaman and later a soldier, fought at The Battle of Blewford, later moved to Cork, Ireland, by 1787. [TNA.AO1237.1]

CROSBIE, THOMAS, a former Sergeant of the 70th [Surrey] Regiment, settled in Bathurst, Ontario, on 2 September 1819. [PAO.ms154]

CROWE, RICHARD ROBERT, from Ireland to America in 1757 as an officer of the 48th [Northamptonshire] Regiment, fought at the Sieges of Quebec, Louisbourg, and Havanna, then settled near Amboy, Monmouth County, New Jersey, in 1763, a Loyalist and British Army officer during the American Revolution, later settled in Parrsburgh, Canada. [UEL.II.1218]

CRUICE, JAMES, a Second Lieutenant of the Walsh Regiment, of the Irish Brigade in French Service, in America between 1778 and 1783. [IS.XIII.51]

CRUMP, HENRY, from Ireland, late private of the 90th [Perthshire] Regiment, settled in Burgess, Ontario, on 18 September 1816. [PAO.ms154]

CRUMP, JOHN, from Ireland, late private of the 90th [Perthshire] Regiment, settled in Burgess, Ontario, on 18 September 1816. [PAO.ms154]

CUFFE, Captain MICHAEL, of the 27th [Inniskilling] Regiment, was appointed Major of the said regiment on 7 April 1777. [SM.40.223]

CULLEN, JAMES, a soldier of the 18th [Royal Regiment of Ireland] Foot in Philadelphia, Pennsylvania, in 1767. [TNA.WO.76/25]

CULLEN, JEREMIAH, born in Ireland, a Lieutenant of the New York Militia, returned to Ireland and died there before 1790. [TNA.AO12.102.217]

CULLEN, MICHAEL, from Ireland, late private of the 8TH [King's] Regiment, settled in Burgess, Ontario, on 30 September 1816. [PAO.ms154]

CUMMINGS, FRANCIS H., from Ireland, late Lieutenant of the 104th [North British] Regiment, settled in Burgess, Ontario, on 31 July 1817. [PAO.ms154]

CUMMINGS, JAMES, a soldier of the 18th [the Royal Regiment of Ireland] Foot, in Philadelphia, Pennsylvania, in 1772. [TNA.WO.76/25]

CUNNINGHAM, WALTER, from Ireland to Anson County, North Carolina, a land surveyor, he joined the British Army in 1778 and was appointed Ensign of the 105th [Volunteers of Ireland] Foot, returned to Belfast, Ireland, by 1783. [TNA.AO1291.45]

CUNNINGHAM, MATTHEW, late private of the Glengarry Fencibles, settled in Drummond, Ontario, on 16 July 1816. [PAO.ms154]

CURRY, JOHN, emigrated to Pennsylvania in 1773, settled in Lancaster County, a Loyalist in Naval service, returned to County Antrim, Ireland, by 1788. [TNA.AO12.42.86]

CURRY, ROBERT, a soldier, made Corporal of the 18th [Royal Regiment of Foot of Ireland] in Charlestown Heights, Massachusetts, in 1775. [TNA.WO.12.3801]

CURTIN, JOHN, born 1695 in County Cork, a soldier of the 48th [Northamptonshire] Regiment of Foot, fought in the French and Indian War, was discharged at Crown Point, New York, on 20 October 1763, was granted land near Lake Champlain which was dispossessed in 1780 as he was a Loyalist. [TNA.WO.116.9; AS12.102.130]

CURTIS, JOSEPH, born 1717 in Ireland, a planter in Augusta, Virginia, enlisted in September 1756, a soldier of Colonel George Washington's Company in August 1757. [VCS]

DALRYMPLE, CHARLES, a soldier of the 18th [Royal Regiment of Ireland] Foot at Charlestown Heights, Massachusetts, in 1775. [TNA.WO12.3501]

DALRYMPLE, Captain WILLIAM, Commandant of the Loyal Irish Volunteers, a long letter from St Fernando de Omao, on the Mosquito Shore, Honduras, dated 21 October 1779. [SM.41.666-673]; Captain commanding the Corps of Foot serving in Jamaica was appointed a Major there, on 21 December 1779. [SM.41.687]

DAILY, JAMES, from Ireland, late of the Royal Sappers, settled in Lanark, Ontario, on 1 November 1820. [PAO.ms154]

DALY, DENNIS, a soldier of Colonel Thornhill's Company in Barbados in 1679. [TNA.CO1.44.47]

DALY, DENNIS, Second Lieutenant of Militia in Montserrat in 1705. [SPAWI.1705.13477]

DALEY, Lieutenant EDMOND, in Montserrat from 1677 to 1678. [TNA]

DALEY, HUGH, from Ireland, late a Sergeant of the 8th [King's] Regiment, settled in Burgess, Ontario, on 20 September 1816. [PAO.ms154]

DALY, HUGH, from Ireland, a former Sergeant Major, settled in Leeds, Ontario, on 30 November 1817. [PAO.ms154

DALY, JOHN, a Captain of Militia on Montserrat in 1705. [SPAWI.1705.1347i]

DALYE, OWEN, a soldier of Lieutenant Colonel John Codrington's Company on Barbados in 1679. [H2.173]

DALEY, ROBERT, born 1799 enlisted in the British Army in Donegal in 1812, discharged in St John in 1818, settled in Dalhousie, Nova Scotia, in 1820. [TNA.WO.25.548]

DANIEL, MICHAEL H., was appointed a Corporal of the 18th [Royal Regiment of Ireland] Foot, in New York on 21 June 1775. [TNA.WO.76/25]

DARCY, JAMES, a Captain of the Walsh Regiment, of the Irish Brigade in French Service, in America between 1778 and 1783. [IS.XIII.51]

DARCY, LOUIS, Second Lieutenant of the Dillon Regiment, of the Irish Brigade in French Service, in America between 1778 and 1783. [IS.XIII.51]

DARELL, PHILIP a Second Lieutenant of the Walsh Regiment, of the Irish Brigade in French Service, in America between 1778 and 1783. [IS.XIII.51]

DAVAN, JOHN, settled as a grocer in New York city, served in the Royal Artillery during the American Revolution, in Cork, Ireland, by 1784. [TNA.AO13.94.19-28]

DAVIES, RICHARD, late a Lieutenant of the 44th [East Essex] Regiment, son of Simon Davies in Cork, died in New Orleans, Louisiana, probate August 1818, PCC. [TNA]

DAVIS, GEORGE, born 1727 in Ireland, a planter in Norfolk, Virginia, a soldier of Captain Robert Spotswood's Company in Fort Young, Virginia, on 4 October 1757. [VCS]

DAVIS, JOHN, a soldier of the 18th [Royal Regiment of Ireland] Foot in Philadelphia in 1770, appointed Corporal on 25 October 1770, in New York in 1775. [TNA.WO.76/25]

DAVIS, THOMAS, a soldier of the 18th [Royal Regiment of Ireland] Foot in Charlestown Heights, Massachusetts, in 1775. [TNA.WO.12.3801]

DAWSON, Lieutenant A.C., in the West Indies and New York, a diary from 1818 until 1821. [PRONI.D618]

DAWSON, GEORGE, an officer of the Royal Irish Artillery, died in the West Indies during March 1794. [IS.XVI]

DAWSON, ROBERT PEEL, Lieutenant of the Grenadier Guards, fought in the 1838 Rebellion in Canada, in 1838 toured the United States, letters between 1838 and 1839. [PRONI.T850]

DE BIRNIERE, JOHN, Lieutenant of the 18th [Royal Irish Regiment] Foot, around 1770. [PEF.153]

DE HAYS, THOMAS, Sub Lieutenant of the Dillon Regiment, of the Irish Brigade in French Service, in America between 1778 and 1783. [IS.XIII.51]

DE LACHEROIS, H., born at Hilden near Lisburn, an Ensign o the 9th Foot in 1756, a Lieutenant in 1759, a Captain Lieutenant in 1770, a Captain in 1771, he retired in1776, and died in Donaghadee in 1829. See his letter from Havanna, Cuba, dated 30 July 1762. [IS.VII.173]

DELAMAR, PATRICK, son of Peter Delamar of Lillean, County West Meath, a Colonel of the Spanish Army for 25 years, in the Philippines and in Port Rico where he died on19 August 1860. [Multyfarnham, County Westmeath, gravestone]

DE LANCY, DANIEL, born in Ireland, settled in Philadelphia, Pennsylvania, in 1758, later in Hillsborough, North Carolina, in 1775, a Loyalist soldier, moved to Wilmot, Nova Scotia, by 1786. [TNA.AO12.65.18]

DE LANCEY, JOHN PETER, Lieutenant of the 18th [Royal Regiment of Ireland] Foot around 1770. [PEF.156]; was promoted to be Captain of the 18th Foot on 29 July 1780, in place of Benjamin Payne. [SM.42.391]

DELANY, DENNIS, a soldier of the 2nd Battalion of the 84th [Royal Highland Emigrants] Regiment, aboard the frigate Raleigh bound from New York to Charleston, South Carolina, in 1780. [NRS.GD174.2405]

DE MANDEVILLE, JAMES, Second Captain of the Dillon Regiment, of the Irish Brigade in French Service, in America between 1778 and 1783. [IS.XIII.51]

DEMPSEY, HENRY, a soldier of Captain Hall's Company in Barbados in 1679. [TNA.CO1.44.47]

DERRY, JOHN, emigrated from Ireland to America in 1743, settled at Venplanks Point, West Chester County, New York, served in Delancey's Corps during the War of Independence, moved to Nova Scotia by 1788. [UEL.II.1216]

DETLOR, VALENTINE, emigrated from Ireland to America in 1756, settled in Camden District, Charlotte County, New York, enlisted with the British at Crown Point, N.Y. in 1776, later moved to Carleton Island and Le Chine, Canada, by 1783. [OBA.916] [UEL.II.1027]

DEVEREUX, JAMES, a shipmaster based in New York City, served as a Loyalist bombardier in New York City, moved to Wexford, Ireland, by 1783. [TNA.AO12.20.]

DICKINSON, WILLIAM, a soldier of the 18th [Royal Regiment of Ireland] Foot in Philadelphia, Pennsylvania, in 1770, a prisoner in New York in 1775. [TNA.W0.76/25]

DILLON, ARTHUR, Colonel of the Dillon Regiment, of the Irish Brigade in French Service, in America between 1778 and 1783. [IS.XIII.51]

DILLON, Lieutenant Colonel Bartholemew, of the Dillon Regiment, of the Irish Brigade in French Service, in America between 1778 and 1783. [IS.XIII.51]

DILLON, PATRICK, born 1767, enlisted in the British Army in Tipperary in 1804, discharged in Newfoundland, settled in Dalhousie, Nova Scotia, in 1820. [TNA.WO.25.548]

DILLON, THEOBALD, Colonel of the Dillon Regiment, of the Irish Brigade in French Service, in America between 1778 and 1783. [IS.XIII.51]

DILLON, THOMAS, Lieutenant of the Dillon Regiment, of the Irish Brigade in French Service, in America between 1778 and 1783. [IS.XIII.51]

DIX, JOHN, a soldier of the 18th [Royal Regiment of Ireland] Foot, in New York in 1774, was transferred on 9 October 1774. [TNA.WO.76/25]

DOCHERTY, EDWARD, born 1732 in Ireland, a tanner in York, Virginia, a soldier of Captain Henry Woodward's Company in Virginia, on 11 September 1757. [VCS]

DOHARTY, WILLIAM, a militiaman of Captain William Allanby's Company in Barbados in 1679. [TNA.CO1.44.47] [HB2.70]

DOLLEN, THOMAS, born 1727 in Ireland, a shoemaker, enlisted as a soldier of the Second Company of Rangers in Virginia on 21 October 1755. [VCS]

DOLLING, JOHN, a soldier of the 18th [Royal Regiment of Ireland] Foot in Philadelphia, Pennsylvania, in 1770, was appointed as a drummer on 25 October 1770. [TNA.W0.76/25]

DOMMER, WILLIAM, a soldier of the 18th [Royal Regiment of Ireland] Foot in Philadelphia, Pennsylvania, in 1770, enlisted on 26 August 1770, deserted on 24 December 1770. [TNA.WO.76/25]

DONACHY, DANIEL, former soldier of the Glengarry Fencibles, settled in Drummond, Ontario, on 16 July 1816. [PAO.ms154]

DONALDSON, HUGH, late of the 6th [Inniskilling Dragoons] Regiment, settled in Bathurst, Ontario, on 7 October 1819. [PAO.ms154]

DONAHOW, DANIEL, a soldier of Captain Samuel Woodward's Company of Militia in Barbados on 8 January 1679. [H2.156]

DONNAHOW, LOUGHLAN, a soldier in Colonel Thornhill's Company on Barbados in 1679. [TNA.CO1.44.47]

DONALLY, MARK, born 1727 in Ireland, a brewer in Augusta, Virginia, a soldier in Major Andrew Lewis's Company in Virginia in 1757. [VCS]

DONGAN, THOMAS, born 1634 son of Sir John Dongan a Jacobite soldier who fled to France in1649, Thomas was appointed a Colonel of the French Army, in 1677 he returned to England where King Charles II promoted him to Major General and in 1682 he became Governor of New York until dismissed in 1688, he died on 14 December 1715.

DONNELLAN, PATRICK, born 1770, enlisted in the British Army in Roscommon in 1804, discharged in 1817, settled in Dalhousie, Nova Scotia, in 1820. [TNA.WO.25.548]

DONNELY, DANIEL, born 1815 in Ireland, a soldier of fortune who was executed in Tampica, Mexico, in 1836. [Macon, Georgia, Telegraph, 7 January 1836]

DONOHOW, DANIEL, a militiaman in Barbados in 1679. [TNA.CO1.44.47]

DONOUGH, TEIGE, a militiaman in Barbados in 1679. [TNA.CO1.44.47]

DONOVAN, DARBY, a soldier of the 2nd Battalion of the 84th [Royal Highland Emigrants Regiment] Foot, aboard the frigate Raleigh bound from New York to Charleston, South Carolina, in 1780. [NRS.GD174.2405]

DONAVAN, JAMES, a Lieutenant of the British Legion, a warrant dated New York in July 1783. [HMC. American. iv.254]

DONOVAN, JOHN, a soldier of Captain Samuel Woodward's Company of Militia in Barbados on 8 January 1679. [H2.156]

DONOVAN, TEIGE, a soldier of Captain Samuel Woodward's Company of Militia in Barbados on 8 January 1679. [H2.156]

DONAHUE, LAUGHLAN, a militiaman in Captain John Sampson's Company on Barbados in 1679. [H2.79]

DORRES, JOHN, born in Ireland, settled in Ninety-six District, South Carolina, before 1776, a Loyalist who bore arms duing the Revolution, moved to Montreal, Canada, by 1786. [TNA.AO12.49.50]

DOUGHERTY, EDWARD, in Boston, Massachusetts, enlisted in the Loyal Irish Volunteers in 1775, in England by 1784. [TNA.AO12.100.111]

DOUGHERTY, JOHN, a cordwainer from Dublin, later a soldier of the 58th [Rutlandshire] Regiment of Foot, was found guilty of robbing an officer's quarters in Quebec and was sentenced to 1000 lashes. [TNA.WO71.46.10-14; WO25.435.67]

DOUGHERTY, JAMES, from Ireland, late of the 4th Veterans Regiment, settled in Drummond, Ontario, on 16 March 1818. [PAO.ms154]

DOWD, ARTHUR, late of the 19th [Yorkshire] Regiment, applied to settle in Canada on 27 May 1827. [TNA.CO384.16]

DOWDALL, LAURENCE, born in Ireland in 1659, a soldier in Flanders, then in Darien, Panama, around 1700, settled in Jamaica, a Colonel of Militia, died 30 January 1743. [Greenwich gravestone, St Andrews, Jamaica]

DOWDY, Sergeant DANIEL, in Montserrat in 1677-1678. [TNA]

DOWNES, WILLIAM, a Major of the Royal Irish Artillery during the French and Indian War, settled in Camden District, South Carolina, in 1762, joined the British Army in SC., fought at the Siege of Charleston, was murdered by the rebels on 15 April 1781. [TNA.AO12.46.240]

DOWELL, TEIGE, a militiaman in Captain John Sampson's Company on Barbados in 1679. [H2.79]

DOYLE, T. HENRY, born 27 February 1794 in County Wexford, Paymaster of the 75th [Prince of Wales] Regiment, married Jemima Ann Younger in Guadaloupe, West Indies, on 13 April 1816. [IG.8.2.273]

DOYLE, J., formerly the Adjutant General of the 105th [Volunteers of Ireland] Foot in South Carolina, settled in Dublin, Ireland, an affidavit, 1783. [TNA.AO.13.125.366-388]

DOYLE, MICHAEL, a soldier of the 2nd Battalion of the 84th [Royal Highland Emigrants] Regiment, aboard the frigate Raleigh bound from New York to Charleston, South Carolina, in 1780. [NRS.GD174.2405]

DOYLE, THOMAS, born in Ireland, a militiaman from Albemarle County, Virginia, deserted the Virginia Regiment in 1757. [VaGaz.347]

DOYLE, WELLBORE ELLIS, born 1758, an officer of the 55th Foot, a Captain Lieutenant by 1777, was Lieutenant Colonel of the Volunteers of Ireland at the Battles of Camden and at Hobkirk's Hill. [IS.VII.153]

DOYLE, Major, a Court of Enquiry re the destruction of Fair Lawn Hospital in Charleston, South Carolina, and the capture of the patients, by the rebels, on 29 January 1782. [HMC. American. ii.387]; at a skirmish on Daniel's Island in February 1782. [HMC. American. ii.403]

DRISCOLL, JEREMIAH, born 1784 in Ireland, late of the 58th [Rutlandshire] Foot, applied to settle in Canada on 12 June 1827. [TNA.CO384.16]

DRUGON, JAMES, a soldier of the 18th [Royal Regiment of Ireland] Foot, in Philadelphia, Pennsylvania, in 1772. [TNA.WO.76/25]

DRUMMOND. Lieutenant Colonel of the 27th [Inniskilling] Regiment, fought the French on St Lucia, West Indies, in May 1756. [IR.47]

DUANE, ANTHONY, born 1682 in Cong, County Galway, the purser of HMS Seaford in New York in 1713, later a merchant in New York, died there in 1747.

DUDSON, JOHN, a soldier of the 18th [Royal Regiment of Ireland] Foot in Philadelphia, Pennsylvania, in 1767. [TNA.WO.76/25]

DUFFY, PATRICK, born 1790, enlisted in the British Army in Roscommon in 1813, discharged in Fredericton, New Brunswick, in 1818, settled in Dalhousie, Nova Scotia, in 1820. [TNA.WO.25.548]

DUGAN, CHARLES, a militiaman in Captain Samuel Woodward's Company in Barbados in 1679. [TNA.CO1.44.47] [H2.156]

DUGGAN, JOHN, Lieutenant of the Dillon Regiment, of the Irish Brigade in French Service, in America between 1778 and 1783. [IS.XIII.51]

DULMAGE, JOHN, emigrated from Ireland to America in 1756, settled in Camden District, Charlotte County, New York, a Loyalist and a Lieutenant of Jessop's Corps, of the King's Loyal Americans, until 1783, then settled in Osswegatchie, Canada. [UEL.II.1088]

DUNBAR, JOHN, from Ireland, formerly a Corporal of the 4th Royal Veteran Battalion, settled in Bathurst, Ontario, on 30 June 1817. [PAO.ms1817]

DUNCAN, JOHN, a soldier of the 18th [Royal Regiment of Ireland] Foot in Philadelphia, Pennsylvania, in 1770; in New York in 1775. [TNA.WO.76/25]

DUNLAP, JOHN, born 1747 in Strabane, County Tyrone, settled in Philadelphia, Pennsylvania, as a printer, he was a Captain of Militia during a rebellion in Western Pennsylvania in 1794, he died in 1812. [PRONI.T.1336.1.22]

DUNN, JOHN, a soldier of the 18th [Royal Regiment of Ireland] Foot in Philadelphia, Pennsylvania, in 1770. [TNA.WO.76/25]

DUNN, JOHN, born 1776, enlisted in the British Army in Queen's County, Ireland, in 1804, discharged in Fredericton, New Brunswick, in 1818, settled in Dalhousie, Nova Scotia, in 1820. [TNA.WO.25.548]

DUN, RICHARD, born 1740 in Ireland, 5 foot 5 inches in height, a labourer, ruddy complexion, grey eyes and brown hair, was recruited in Boston, Massachusetts, by Ensign John Archbold of the 40th [Somerset] Regiment, on 19 January 1758. [NRS.GD45.2.35.9]

DUNSMORE, DAVID, emigrated from Ireland to America in 1765, settled in Ninety-six District, South Carolina, by 1775, a Loyalist soldier during the American Revolution, later settled in Rawdon, Nova Scotia. [UEL.I.171]

DUTSON, JOHN, a Sergeant of the 18th [Royal Regiment of Ireland] Foot, in Charlestown Heights, Massachusetts, in 1775. [TNA.WO.12.3801]

DYER, DANIEL, formerly a soldier of the 18th [Royal Regiment of Ireland] Foot, then of the 23rd [Royal Welsh] Regiment, surrendered at Yorktown, Virginia, in 1783

EASDALE, SAMUEL, born 1722 in Ireland, an Indian trader in Frederick, Virginia, a soldier in Major Andrew Lewis's Company in Virginia in 1757. [VCS]

ECKLIN, THOMAS, from Ireland, a former Corporal of the 5th Dragoon Guards, settled in Bathurst, Ontario, on 7 August 1817. [PAO.ms154]

EDMONSTONE, CHARLES, Captain or Captain Lieutenant of the 18th [Royal Regiment of Ireland] Foot, to Fort Pitt, Ohio, in 1767; Captain of the 18th Foot in Philadelphia, Pennsylvania, in 1767. [TNA.WO.76/25][PEF.13/113]

ELDER, ROBERT, emigrated from Ireland to Pennsylvania in 1772, he moved to Camden District, South Carolina, in 1775, joined the Militia in 1780, returned to Ireland and settled in County Antrim, Ireland, by 1783. [TNA.AO12.48.195-200]

ELLIOT, JOHN, a former Lieutenant of the Royal Marines, settled in Bathurst, Ontario, on 18 September 1819. [PAO.ms154]

ELLIOT, ..., an Ensign of Lord Blakeney's Regiment, was wounded at the Siege of Ticonderoga, New York, in July 1758. [NRS]

ELLIOT, ..., a former Lieutenant of the Royal Marines, settled in Bastard, Ontario, on 29 September 1819. [PAO.ms154]

ELLIS, JOHN JOYNER, Lieutenant of the 18th [Royal Regiment of Ireland] Foot around 1770. [PEF.160]

ELLIS, NATHANIEL, from Ireland, late a private of the 49th [Hertfordshire] Regiment, settled in Bathurst, Ontario, on 10 September 1818. [PAO.ms154]

EMBURY, JOHN, born in Ireland, settled in Charlotte County, New York, a Loyalist soldier from 1776, settled in Montreal, Quebec, by 1783. [UEL.II.917]

ENGLISH, JOHN, late of the Glengarry Regiment, settled in Drummond, Ontario, on 22 August 1816. [PAO.ms154]

ENGLISH, JOHN, late of the104th [North British Regiment] Foot, settled in Burgess, Ontario, on 22 August 1816. [PAO.ms154]

ENNIS, TEAGE, a militiaman in HM Guards of Barbados in 1679. [TNA.CO1.44.47]

ENNIS, JOHN, a militiaman in Captain Timothy Thornhill's Company on Barbados in 1679. [H2.80]

ERWIN, JOHN, a Corporal of the 18th [Royal Regiment of Ireland] Foot, in New York in 1775. [TNA.WO.75/25]

EVANS, JOHN, Captain or Captain Lieutenant of the 18th [Royal Regiment of Ireland] Foot around 1770. [PEF.117]

EVAN, NICHOLAS, Lieutenant of the Dillon Regiment, of the Irish Brigade in French Service, in America between 1778 and 1783. [IS.XIII.51]

EVANS THOMAS, a soldier of the 27th [Inniskilling] Regiment, at Fort George, New York, on 4 September 1757. [NRS.GD45.2.35.2]

EVATT, HENRT, from Ireland, a former Lieutenant of the 21st [Royal North British Fusiliers] Regiment, settled in Young, Ontario, on 18 August 1818. [PAO.ms154]

FALLON, PATRICK, in Killashee, County Longford, an army pensioner, applied to settle in Canada on17 March 1827. [TNA.CO384.16]

FARRELL, EDWARD, from Ireland, a former private of the 4th Dragoon Guards, settled in Bathurst, Ontario, on 31 July 1817. [PAO.ms154]

FARRELL, EDWARD, in Kilmainham Royal Hospital in Dublin, for 12 years in the 24th [Warwick] Foot, applied to settle in Canada on 15 August 1827. [TNA.CO384.16]

FARRELL, FRANCIS, a soldier of the 18th [Royal Regiment of Ireland] Foot, in Philadelphia, Pennsylvania, in 1770. [TNA.WO.76/25]

FARRELL, JAMES, born 1813 in Ireland, settled in Green County, New York, a soldier of fortune, was executed in Tampica, Mexico, in 1836. [Macon, Georgia, Telegraph, 7 January 1836]

FENNELL, JOHN, Second Lieutenant of the Dillon Regiment, of the Irish Brigade in French Service, in America between 1778 and 1783. [IS.XIII.51]

FENTON, JACOB, a soldier of the 18th [Royal Regiment of Ireland] Foot in Charlestown Heights, Massachusetts, in 1775. [TNA.WO.12.3801]

FENTON, JOHN, an officer of the Queen's Royal Irish Regiment in America during the French and Indian Wars, Captain of Fort William and Mary in Portsmouth, New Hampshire, in 1775, a Loyalist who died in Dublin, Ireland, in 1785. [TNA.AO12.101.215]

FERMOR, HENRY, Captain or Captain Lieutenant of the 18th [Royal Regiment of Ireland] Foot around 1770. [PEF.118]

FERNS, JONATHAN GORE, former Major of the 76th Regiment of Foot, eldest son of T. Burgh Ferns in County Dublin, died in Halifax, Nova Scotia, on 26 May 1856. [GM.ns2.1.124]

FERRIER, JOHN, in Magherafelt, County Londonderry, late a gunner of the Royal Artillery, applied to settle in Canada on 24 March 1827. [TNA.CO384.16]

FIELD, HENRY, born 1734 in Ireland, a cordiner in Augusta, Virginia, a soldier of Captain Henry Woodward's Company in Virginia, on 11 September 1757. [VCS]

FIELD, WILLIAM, born 1715 in Ireland, a farmer who enlisted in the Second Company of Rangers in Virginia on 21 October 1755. [VCS]

FIELDING, PATRICK, a soldier of the 2nd Battalion of the 84th [Royal Highland Emigrants] Regiment, aboard the frigate Raleigh bound from New York to Charleston, South Carolina, in 1780. [NRS.GD174.2405]

FINDLAND, DARBY, a militiaman in Captain John Sampson's Company on Barbados in 1679. [H2.79]

FINDLAND, TEIGE, a militiaman in Captain John Sampson's Company on Barbados in 1679. [H2.79]

FINDLEY, BRIANT, born 1735 in Ireland, a butcher in Augusta, Virginia, a soldier of Captain Henry Woodward's Company in Virginia, on 11 September 1757. [VCS]

FINNARTY, JOHN, formerly of the 4th Royal Veteran Battalion, settled in Bathurst, Ontario, on 30 June 1817. [PAO.ms154]

FINNY, JAMES, from Ireland, a former private of the 19th Dragoons, settled in Elmsley, Ontario, on 23 October 1817. [PAO.ms154]

FITZGERALD, EDWARD, Sub Lieutenant of the Dillon Regiment, of the Irish Brigade in French Service, in America between 1778 and 1783. [IS.XIII.51]

FITZGERALD, GERALD, Lieutenant of the 2nd Battalion of the 84th [Royal Highland Emigrants] Regiment at Quebec in 1777. [SM.39.456]

FITZGERALD, JAMES, born 1731 in Ireland, a planter in Augusta, Virginia, enlisted in August 1756, a soldier in Colonel George Washington's Company in 1757. [VCS]

FITZGERALD, JAMES, from Ireland, formerly in the Royal Navy, settled in Beckwith, Ontario, on 9 September 1817. [PAO.ms154]

FITZGERALD, JOHN, from Ireland, formerly a private of the Glengarry Fencibles, settled in Burgess, Ontario, on 26 September 1816. [PAO.ms154]

FITZMAURICE, JOSEPH, Sub Lieutenant of the Dillon Regiment, of the Irish Brigade in French Service, in America between 1778 and 1783. [IS.XIII.51]

FITZGERALD, MICHAEL, a soldier of the 2nd Battalion of the 84th [Royal Highland Emigrants] Regiment, aboard the frigate Raleigh bound from New York to Charleston, South Carolina, in 1780. [NRS.GD174.2405]

FITZGERALD, PATRICK, a former Corporal of the York Chasseurs, settled in Bathurst, Ontario, on 22 September 1819. [PAO.ms154]

FITZGERALD, PATRICK, from Ireland, formerly of the Prince of Wales's Chasseurs, settled in Beckwith, Ontario, on 10 October 1820. [PAO.ms154]

FITZGERALD, WILLIAM, born 1729 in Ireland, a weaver in Frederick, Virginia, enlisted in December 1756, a soldier in Colonel George Washington's Company in 1757. [VCS]

FITZGERALD, Captain WILLIAM, ARBUCKLE, of the Amelia County, Militia, Virginia, in 1761. [VCS]

FITZGERALD, WILLIAM, born 1737 in Ireland, dark complexion and dark eyes, 5 foot seven inches, a labourer, was recruited in Boston, Massachusetts, by Captain Cosnan of the 45th [Nottinghamshire] Regiment of Foot, on 2 January 1758. [NRS.GD45.2.24.4B]

FITZGERALD, ..., a soldier of the 2nd Battalion of the 84th [Royal Highland Emigrants] Regiment, aboard the frigate Raleigh bound from New York to Charleston, South Carolina, in 1780. [NRS.GD174.2405]

FITZHARRIS, WILLIAM, Second Lieutenant of the Dillon Regiment, of the Irish Brigade in French Service, in America between 1778 and 1783. [IS.XIII.51]

FITZHUGH, ..., a Cornet, a letter, dated 1779. [HMC. American. ii.25]

FITZMAURICE, THOMAS, a Captain of the Walsh Regiment, of the Irish Brigade in French Service, in America between 1778 and 1783. [IS.XIII.51]

FITZMAURICE, ULYSSES, from Ireland, a former Lieutenant of the Canadian Fusiliers, settled in Bathurst, Ontario, on 30 June 1817. [PAO.ms154]

FITZPATRICK, JOHN, born 1711 in Ireland, a clothier who enlisted in Captain William Bronaugh's Company, in Alexandria, Virginia, in December 1754. [VCS]

FITZPATRICK, PETER, born in Ireland, emigrated to America in 1766, settled in the Mohawk Valley, Tryon County, New York, a Loyalist soldier in the 2nd Battalion of Sir John Johnson's Regiment [King's Royal Regiment of New York] from 1776 until 1783, moved to Canada by 1784. [UEL.II.1017]

FITZSIMMONS, ULYSSES, from Ireland, a former Lieutenant of the Canadian Fencibles, settled in Burgess, Ontario, on 19 September 1816. [PAO.ms154]

FLANAGAN, DANIEL, a soldier of the 18th [Royal Regiment of Ireland] Foot in Philadelphia, Pennsylvania, in 1770, enlisted on 26 April 1770, deserted on 5 September 1770. [TNA.WO.76/25]

FLEMING, WILLIAM, in Fintown, County Tyrone, formerly a Corporal of the 12th [East Suffolk] Foot, applied to settle in Canada on 15 January 1826. [TMA.CO384.16]

FLYN, ANDREW, a cooper from Fermanagh, a soldier of the 58th [Rutlandshire] Regiment of Foot, was acquitted of robbery in Quebec, deserted on 22 January 1764. [TNA.WO25.435/67-8, 85-6]

FLYNN, DENNIS, a soldier of the 18th [Royal Regiment of Ireland] Foot in Charlestown Heights, Massachusetts, in 1775. [TNA.WO.12.3801]

FLYNN, JAMES, a soldier of the 18th [Royal Regiment of Ireland] Foot, was killed at Bunker Hill, Massachusetts, in 1775

FLYNN, WILLIAM, emigrated from Ireland to New York City in 1763, he served in the Commissary General's department during the war, moved to Halifax, Nova Scotia, by 1786, from there to London in 1787. [TNA.AO12.102.96]

FOGARTY, DANIEL, a soldier of an Independent Company in St Kitts, in 1689. [SPAWI.1689.65i]

FOLEY, JOHN, from Ireland, late of the Glengarry Fencibles, settled in Bathurst, Ontario, on 23 July 1816. [PAO.ms154]

FOLLIOT, HENRY, Field Officer of the 18th [Royal Regiment of Ireland] Foot, around 1770. [PEF.79]

FORBES, Lord, Captain General of the Leeward Islands, papers, 1731. [Castle Forbes archive, Newtonmore]

FORD, PHILLIP, a soldier of the 18th [The Royal Regiment of Ireland] Foot, in Philadelphia, Pennsylvania, deserted on 5 July 1771. [TNA.WO.76/75]

FORDU, JOSEPH, a soldier of the 18th [Royal Regiment of Ireland] Foot in Charlestown Heights, Massachusetts, in 1775. [TNA.WO.12.3801]

FORREST, JAMES, a merchant in Boston, Massachusetts, an officer of the Loyal Irish Volunteers in 1775. [TNA.AO12.74.319]

FOWLER, ALEXANDER, Lieutenant of the 18th [Royal Regiment of Ireland] Foot, at New York in 1775, died in Canada in 1780. [OBA] [PEF.162]

FOWLER, THOMAS, born 1738 in Ireland, 5 feet 5 inches tall, thick set, dark eyes and a red complexion, deserted from the Virginia Regiment on 2 June 1759. [MG.740]

FRIEL, JOHN, emigrated from Ireland to America in 1763, settled in Johnstown, Tryon County, New York, a Loyalist soldier.

FROST, EDWARD, emigrated from Ireland to America in 1754, a soldier under Sir William Johnson [the King's Royal Regiment of New York] during the French and Indian War, settled in Tryon County, New York, a Loyalist and a soldier in Sir John Johnson's Regiment, [the King's Royal Regiment of New York] from 1776 until 1783, then settled in the 5th Township, New Johnston, Quebec. [UEL.I.354]

FULLEN, PETER, from Ireland, late a private of the 27th [Inniskilling] Foot, settled in Beckwith, Ontario, on 3 September 1820. [PAO.ms154]

FULLAN, THOMAS, of 22 Union Street, Belfast, late a Sergeant of the 27th [Inniskilling] Foot, applied to settle in Canada on 17 April 1827. [TNA.CO384.16]

FULTON, JAMES, from Ireland, late a Corporal of the 12th Royal Veteran Battalion, settled in Beckwith, Ontario, on 3 September 1820. [PAO.ms154]

GAFFNEY, NICHOLAS, a soldier of the 18th [Royal Regiment of Ireland] Foot in Philadelphia, Pennsylvania, in 1767, at

Charleston Heights, Massachusetts, in 1775. [TNA.WO.76/25; WO.12.3501]

GAHAGAN, BRYANT, born 1722 in Ireland, a planter in Augusta, Virginia, a soldier of Captain Robert Spotswood's Company in Fort Young, Virginia, on 4 October 1757. [VCS]

GAIN, JOHN, from Ireland, late of the Royal Sappers, settled in Lanark, Ontario, on 1 November 1820. [PAO.ms154]

GALLAGHER, HUGH, from Ireland, formerly of the 4th Royal Veteran Battalion, settled in Drummond, Ontario, on 25 September 1817. [PAO.ms154]

GALLOWAY, FRANCIS, born in Ireland, late of the 1st Pennsylvania Battalion recently from the Siege of Ticonderoga, New York, absconded from a Pennsylvanian armed boat in March 1777. [PaEP.331]

GALWAY, DAVID, a planter on Montserrat in 1660s, a Major of Militia there in 1670s. [TNA]

GARVEY, ALEXANDER, a former soldier later an indentured servant, who absconded from Jane Jameson in Kent County, Maryland, in November 1755. [MG.552]

GARVIN, JAMES, formerly a Corporal of the Royal Artillery, settled in Drummond, Ontario, on 1 November 1816. [PAO.ms154]

GEORGE, JOSHUA, an officer of the Royal Irish Artillery, was killed in the West Indies on 21 June 1794. [IS.XVI]

GIBBON, JOHN, a soldier of the 18th [Royal Regiment of Ireland] Foot in Philadelphia, Pennsylvania, in 1770; in New York in 1775. [TNA.WO.76/25]

GILL, EDWARD, born 1731 in Ireland, a joiner in Dinwiddie, Virginia, enlisted in September 1755, a soldier of Colonel George Washington's Company in August 1757. [VCS]

GILL, JAMES, a soldier of the 18th [Royal Regiment of Ireland] Foot, in Philadelphia, Pennsylvania, in 1770; in New York in 1775. [TNA.WO.76/25]

GILL, JOHN, born 1731 in Ireland, a tanner and currier who was recruited for William Cox's Rangers in Virginia On 21 October 1755. [VCS]

GILLESPIE, ..., of the Volunteers of Ireland Regiment, was wounded in South Carolina in 1780. [SM.42.488], died in Ruthwell, Dumfries-shire, Scotland, on 15 June 1818. [SM.82.294]

GILLESPIE, JOHN, late of the Royal Sappers, settled in Lanark, Ontario, on 1 November 1820. [PAO.ms154]

GILLMORE, GEORGE, born in Ireland, was educated at Edinburgh University, a Presbyterian minister in Volumtown, Connecticut, before 1775, a military chaplain at Sorel, Quebec, in 1782. [TNA.AO12.23.56]

GILMORE, JOHN, born 1730 in Ireland, a farmer in Augusta, Virginia, a soldier in Major Andrew Lewis's Company in Virginia in 1757. [VCS]

GLASGOW, SAMUEL, settled in Ninety Sixth District of South Carolina, a Loyalist soldier in the Carolinas, by 1784 he was residing in Cookstown, County Tyrone, Ireland. [TNA.AO12.100.108]

GLEASON, MICHAEL, from Ireland, a former private of the Glengarry Fencibles, settled in Burgess, Ontario, on 30 June 1817. [PAO.ms154]

GOODMAN, MOSES, from Ireland, formerly a Sergeant of the Canadian Fencibles, settled in Burgess, Ontario, on 22 August 1816. [PAO.ms154]

GOODWIN, WILLIAM, a Sergeant, drummer and fifer of the 18th [Royal Regiment of Ireland] Foot in Charleston Heights, Massachusetts, in 1775. [TNA.WO.12.3801]

GORAN, PATRICK, a militiaman in Captain John Sampson's Company on Barbados in 1679. [H2.79]

GORDON, ROBERT, emigrated from Ireland to Philadelphia, Pennsylvania, in 1769, settled in Albany County, and later Tryon County, New York, a Sergeant in Sir John Johnston's Regiment, [King's Royal Regiment of New York] from 1777 to 1783, moved to Canada. [TNA.AO12.28.374]

GORDON, ROBERT, emigrated from Ireland to America around 1770, settled in Pennsylvania, a Loyalist and a soldier, later a Sergeant, in Sir John Johnson's Regiment, [the King's Royal

Regiment of New York], from 1776 until 1783, settled at La Chine, Quebec, in 1783. [UEL.II.993]

GORDON, ..., a Captain of Lord Blakeney's Regiment, was wounded at the Siege of Ticonderoga, New York, in July 1758. [NRS]

GORE, MANLEY, Deputy Ordnance Storekeeper, youngest son of Lieutenant Colonel Gore of Barrowmount, County Kilkenny, Ireland, died in Quebec on 9 May 1835. [GA.35.5093]

GORMAN, CORNELIUS, late of the Royal Sappers, settled in Lanark, Ontario, on 1 November 1820. [PAO.ms154]

GORMAN, HUGH, a militiaman in Barbados in 1679. [TNA.CO1.44.47]

GOWDY, JAMES, surgeon's mate of the 27th [Inniskilling] Regiment was appointed as is surgeon on 4 March 1777 in place of Thomas Harris. [SM.39.167]

GRACE, JOHN, from Ireland, a former private of the 4th Royal Veteran Battalion, settled in Drummond, Ontario, on 25 September 1817. [PAO.ms154]

GRADY, NEIL, late of the Prince of York's Chasseurs, settled in Bathurst, Ontario, on 7 October 1819. [PAO.ms154]

GRAHAM, HENRY, from Ireland, a former Lieutenant of the 103rd Regiment, settled in Drummond. Ontario, on 21 September 1819. [PAO.ms154]

GRANT, JASPER, from Kilmurry, County Cork, an Ensign of the 4th [King's Own] Foot,later he transferred to the 70th [Surrey] Foot, and finally to the 41st [Welch] Foot as Major, he fought in the West Indies in 1796-1797, in 1800 he was sent to Canada with the 41st [Welch] Foot where he was C.O. of Fort George near Niagara, and at Fort Malden hear Amhertssburg in 1806, he died on 5 March 1812 in Ireland. [NLI.Usher pp] [DCB]

GRANT, JOHN, born 1736 in Ireland, a drummer who enlisted in Captain Thomas Cocke's Company, in Williamsburg, Virginia, on 5 December 1755. [VCS]

GREEN, HENRY, emigrated from Ireland to America around 1768, settled at Rawdon, South Carolina, a soldier of the local

Militia later in the British Army as a blacksmith, settled in Canada by 1786. [PAO.LC594][UEL.II.709]

GREEN, JOHN, born 1727 in Ireland, a farmer in Augusta, Virginia, a soldier in Major Andrew Lewis's Company in Virginia in 1757. [VCS]

GREEN, JOHN, a soldier of the 18th [Royal Regiment of Ireland] Foot in Charleston Heights, Massachusetts, in 1775. [TNA.WO.12.3801]

GREENLAW, JOHN BERNARD, Lieutenant of the Dillon Regiment, of the Irish Brigade in French Service, in America between 1778 and 1783. [IS.XIII.51]

GREGORY, JOSEPH, a soldier of the 18th [Royal Regiment of Ireland] Foot in Philadelphia, Pennsylvania, in 1767. [TNA.WO.76/25]

GREGORY, THOMAS, a soldier of the 18th [Royal Regiment of Ireland] Foot, in Philadelphia, Pennsylvania, in 1770, in New York was transferred on 9 October 1774. [TNA.WO.76/25]

GRIFFITH, EDWARD, from Ireland, a former private of the 10th [North Lincoln] Regiment, settled in Beckwith, Ontario, on 13 October 1817. [PAO.ms154]

GRIFFITH, EVAN, from Ireland, a former private of the 81st [Lincolnshire] Regiment, settled in Drummond, Ontario, on 21 October 1816. [PAO.ms154]

GRIFFON, EDWARD, a soldier of the 18th [Royal Regiment of Ireland] Foot in Charlestown Heights, Massachusetts, in 1775. [TNA.WO.12.3801]

GRINFIELD, General WILLIAM, born 1744, Colonel of the 83rd [County Dublin] Regiment, Commander in Chief of the Leeward and Windward Islands in 1802, died on 19 November 1803, husband of Emma Maria Brocas, born 1744, daughter of Reverend John Brocas in Killala, Ireland, died 16 November 1803. [St Michael's gravestone]

GUIN, JAMES, born 1709, a shoemaker, deserted from the Virginia Regiment in 1754. [MG.467]

GUIRON, THOMAS, from Ireland, a former soldier, settled in Drummond, Ontario. On 14 October 1816. [PAO.ms154]

GUNSHINIAN, JAMES, in Killashee, County Longford, an army pensioner, applied to settle in Canada on 17 March 1827. [TNA.CO384.16]

HACKETT, THOMAS, born 1792, enlisted in the British Army in King's County, Ireland, in 1816, discharged in Fredericton, New Brunswick, settled in Dalhousie, Nova Scotia, in 1820. [TNA.WO.25.548]

HAGARTY, JOHN, from Ireland, a former gunner in the Royal Artillery, settled in Bathurst, Ontario, on 30 June 1817. [PAO.ms154]

HAGERTY, MATTHEW, born 1725 in Ireland, enlisted in Captain Christopher Gist's Company in Frederick, Virginia, on 3 June 1756. [VCS]

HALL, JAMES, a former Corporal of the Sappers and Miners, settled in Burgess, Ontario, on 18 September 1819. [PAO.ms154]

HALL, NICHOLAS, a private of the Glengarry Fencibles, settled in Drummond, Ontario, on 16 July 1816. [PAO.ms154]

HAMILTON, HENRY, born 1734 possibly in Dublin, an Ensign, later Lieutenant, of the 15th [East Yorkshire] Regiment of Foot in 1755, fought at Louisbourg, Quebec, and the West Indies, he commanded Crown Point, New York, in 1766, later, in Montreal, Quebec, he resigned his commission in 1775. [DCB]

HAMILTON, ISAAC, Field Officer of the18th Regiment, around 1770, Major of the 18th [Royal Regiment of Ireland] Foot in Philadelphia, Pennsylvania, on 31 October 1772. [TNA.WO2.76/25] [PEF.81]

HAMILTON, JAMES, born about 1753, emigrated from Ireland to Pennsylvania around 1761, moved to Maryland, a Loyalist soldier from 1780, fought at the battles of Hanging Rock, Camden, and Guilford, returned to Ireland via Charleston. [UEL.II.1123]

HAMILTON, JAMES, from Ireland to Rowan County, North Carolina, a Captain of the South Carolina Volunteers, moved to Monaghan, Ireland, by 1785. [TNA.AO12.71.166]

HAMILTON, JAMES, late of the Royal Navy, emigrated via Cork aboard the Stakesby bound for Quebec, landed there on 2 September 1823. [CC.10.9.1823]

HAMILTON, JOHN, born 1737 in Ireland, a planter in Frederick, Virginia, enlisted in July 1757, a soldier of Colonel George Washington's Company in August 1757. [VCS]

HAMILTON, JOHN, emigrated from Ireland to America, settled at Coty Creek, Ninety-six District, South Carolina, a Loyalist militiaman, later moved to Patago Jack River, Cumberland, in 1783. [UEL.II.842]

HAMILTON, JOHN, born 1732 in Ireland, a weaver who enlisted in Captain Thomas Cocke's Company in Fredericksburg, Virginia, on 10 October 1755. [VCS]

HAMILTON, JOHN, settled in Virginia and North Carolina as a merchant, Colonel of the 96th Militia, settled in Monaghan, Ireland, by 1785. [TNA.AO12.71.166]

HAMILTON, OTHO, born 1688, former Major of the 40th [Somerset] Regiment, Lieutenant Governor of Placientia in Newfoundland, died in Waterford, Ireland, on 7 February 1770. [SM.32.111]

HAMILTON, ROBERT, Captain or Captain Lieutenant of the 18th [Royal Regiment of Ireland] Foot around 1770. [PEF.119]

HAMMILL, DANIEL, emigrated from Ireland to America before 1770, a schoolmaster in Dutchess County, New York, a Loyalist soldier from 1777, settled in Annapolis, Nova Scotia, by 1783. [TNA.AO12.19.319]

HAND, EDWARD, born 1744 in King's County [now Offaly, Ireland], was educated at Trinity College in Dublin, emigrated via Cork to Philadelphia in 1767, a Staff Officer of the 18th [Royal Regiment of Ireland] Foot, a surgeon's mate of the Royal Regiment of Ireland, at Fort Pitt, Ohio, in 1771, settled in Pennsylvania, a Lieutenant Colonel of the Pennsylvania Regiment, later a Brigadier at the Siege of Yorktown, Virginia. [TNA.WO12.3801], died on 3 September 1802.

HANDFORD, HENRY, a soldier of the 18th [Royal Regiment of Ireland] Foot in Philadelphia, Pennsylvania, in 1767. [TNA.WO.76/25]; a soldier of the Royal Regiment of Ireland, at Charleston Heights, Massachusetts, in 1775. [TNA.WO12.3501]

HANDEMEDE, JOHN, Staff Officer of the 18th [Royal Irish Regiment] Foot around 1770. [PEF.207]

HANDLEY, THOMAS, a soldier of the 18th [Royal Regiment of Ireland] Foot in Charlestown Heights, Massachusetts, in 1775. [TNA.WO.12.3801]

HANLEY, JOHN, drummer of the 18th [Royal Regiment of Ireland] Foot, in Philadelphia, Pennsylvania, in 1770. [TNA.WO.76/25]

HANNAN, ANTHONY, born 1776, enlisted in the British Army in Tipperary, in 1804, discharged in Newfoundland in 1818, settled in Dalhousie, Nova Scotia, in 1820. [TNA.WO.25.548]

HARBINSON, WILLIAM, a soldier of the 18th [Royal Regiment of Ireland] Foot in Philadelphia, Pennsylvania, in 1770, was transferred to Captain Evan's Company and promoted to Corporal on 24 October 1770. [TNA.WO.76/25]

HARDING, GEORGE, emigrated from Ireland to America in 1765, a house carpenter in Philadelphia, Pennsylvania, a Loyalist soldier, later settled in Shelbourne, Nova Scotia, by 1783. [OBA.472]

HARDING, WILLIAM, emigrated from Ireland to settle between Augusta and Savannah, Georgia, in 1768, later in Queensborough, a Captain of Militia, died in July 1776. [TNA.AO13.35.391]

HARDMAN, JOHN, born 1743 in County Cavan, enlisted in the 22nd [Cheshire] Regiment of Foot, a drummer who was wounded at the Siege of Louisbourg, Acadia, in 1758, served throughout the American Revolution, was discharged in 1787. [TNA.WO.121.1; 17.124]

HARPER, CHARLES, a soldier of the 18th [Royal Regiment of Ireland] Foot, in New York in 1775. [TNA.WO76/25]

HARPER, ROBERT, a Lieutenant of the 27th [Inniskilling] Foot, 1849. [NRS.CS3.4.304]

HARRINGTON, DERMOT, a soldier of Captain Thornhill's Company on Barbados in 1679. [TNA.CO1.44.47]

HARRIS, THOMAS CATHCART, an officer of the Royal Irish Artillery, died in the West Indies on 31 May 1794. [IS.XVI]

HART, ROGER, a prisoner of war in St Domingo, a will dated 1788. [PWI]

HARVEY, JOHN, a soldier of the 18th [Royal Regiment of Ireland] Foot in New York in 1775. [TNA.WO.76/25]

HASTINGS, FRANCIS [later RAWDON],was born 1754 in County Down, an Ensign of the 71st [Highland] Regiment in 1771, sent to America in 1774 as a Lieutenant of the 5th [Royal

Northumberland] Foot, later Captain of the 63rd [West Suffolk] Regiment, fought at the Battles of Bunker Hill, Monmouth, and Hobkirk's Hill, Colonel of the Volunteers of Ireland, a Loyalist unit he raised in 1779, he died in 1826.

HAVILAND, WILLIAM, born in Ireland, an Ensign of the 43rd [Monmouthshire Regiment] of Foot in 1739, fought at the Siege of Cartagena in Columbia in 1741, in 1757 he brought the 27th [Inniskilling Regiment from New York to besiege Louisbourg, Acadia, in 1758 he was in the attack on Fort Carillon, Quebec, and later on Montreal, Quebec, in 1760 as Colonel of the 60th [Royal American] Regiment] he was at Martinique and the Siege of Havanna, Cuba, in 1762. [DCB]

HAY, JAMES, late Major of the 18th [Inniskilling] Regiment, 16 December 1793. [NRS.CS97.1129]

HAYES, THOMAS, from Ireland, late of the Prince of York's Chasseurs, settled in Beckwith, Ontario, on 21 October 1819. [PAO.ms154]

HAYS, NICHOLAS, a soldier stationed at Placentia, Newfoundland, in 1732. [TNA.CO194.24.109]

HAYWOOD, THOMAS, a soldier of the 18th [Royal Regiment of Ireland] Foot, arrived in Philadelphia, Pennsylvania, in July 1767, deserted on 13 September 1768 in Philadelphia, returned to his regiment, moved to New York City in 1774, was transferred to the 52nd [Oxfordshire] Regiment, later was sent with the 49th [Hertfordshire] Regiment to the West Indies.

HEALY, PATRICK, born 1741 in Ireland, brown complexion, strongly made and black hair, a labourer, was recruited in Boston, Massachusetts, by Ensign John Archbold of the 40th [Somerset] Regiment, on 19 January 1758. [NRS.GD45.2.35.9]

HEASLIP, JAMES, emigrated from Ireland to America in 1774, settled at Beaver Dam near Albany, New York, served as a Corporal of Butler's Rangers, later in Quebec by 1787. [OBA.818] [UEL.II.965]

HENNESY, JOHN, settled in Charleston, South Carolina, a Loyalist who served in the Quartermaster's Department, returned to Ireland in 1787. [PROS.AO12.47/244]

HENRY, BARTHOLEMEW, emigrated from Ireland to America, settled in Reading Township, Little York County, Pennsylvania, around 1770, a Loyalist soldier, returned to Londonderry, Ireland, by 1783. [TNA.AO12.100.328]

HENRY, WILLIAM, emigrated from Killeleagh, County Down, Ireland to America, settled in Reading Chester County, Pennsylvania, around 1770, a Loyalist soldier, returned to Killeleagh, Ireland, by 1783. [TNA.AO12.100.339]

HERON, ISAAC, emigrated from Ireland to America in 1763, a watchmaker in New York City, an officer of the Artillery Militia of New York from 1773, served during the American Revolution, moved to Cork, Ireland, a memorial dated 1787. [TNA.AO12.24.203]

HEWETSON, THOMAS WALLIS, possibly from Kilkenny, Ireland, a Lieutenant of the Royal Marines, died in Boston, Massachusetts, probate, May 1777, PCC. [TNA]

HEWITT, WILLIAM, possibly from Cork, a former surgeon and Ensign of the 25th [King's Own Scottish Borderers] Foot, then residing in Charleston, South Carolina, probate 25 March 1773, S.C.

HIBBARD, RICHARD, a soldier of the 18th [Royal Regiment of Ireland] Foot in Charlestown Heights, Massachusetts, in 1775. [TNA.WO.12.3801]

HICKEY, MATTHEW, a soldier stationed at Placentia, Newfoundland, in 1732. [TNA.CO194.24.109]

HICKEY, WILLIAM, a soldier stationed at Placentia, Newfoundland, in 1732. [TNA.CO194.24.109]

HIGGINS, JAMES, born in Drumard, County Londonderry, a weaver, dyer, and farmer in Danbury, Connecticut, a Loyalist soldier in 1777. [TNA.AO.12.99.31]

HIGGINS, JOHN, born in Drumard, County Londonderry, a farmer in Danbury, Connecticut, a Loyalist soldier in 1777, was killed at the Battle of Bennington. [TNA.AO.12.99.31]

HIGGINS, LAURENCE, born 1715 in Ireland, a planter who was recruited for William Cox's Rangers in Virginia on 16 October 1755. [VCS]

HILL, JOHN, emigrated from Ireland to New York in 1773, moved to Boston, Massachusetts, after 1775, a Captain of the Royal Marines. [UEL.I.585]

HILL, SAMUEL, born 1723 in Ireland, a weaver who was recruited into Stewart's Light Horse in Virginia on 28 December 1755. [VCS]

HILL, SAMUEL, from the north of Ireland, settled at Long Cane, South Carolina, an Ensign with the Militia, moved to Jamaica in 1783, died in Surrey, England, in 1786. [TNA.AO12.48.195]

HILLDEBRAND, JACOB, a soldier of the 18th [Royal Regiment of Ireland] Foot in Philadelphia, Pennsylvania, in 1767. [TNA.WO.76/25]; a soldier of the 18th [Royal Regiment of Ireland] Foot at Charleston Heights, Massachusetts, in 1775. [TNA.WO12.3501]

HINDMAN, SAMUEL, born in Ireland, emigrated to America in 1762, settled at White Creek, Charlotte County, New York, an Ensign of the Queen's Rangers from 1777, later moved to Chambly and at the Bay of Chaleur by 1783. [UEL.II.990]

HINGSTON, EBENEZER MURDOCH, son of Reverend James Hingston in Ireland, settled in Freehold, New Jersey, he joined the army at Trenton, New Jersey, in 1776, an army guide, in 1780 with his wife and family sailed from New York to Ireland. [TNA.AO12.13.96.501-505]

HIROLYHY, Lieutenant Colonel TIMOTHY, from Ireland to America in 1753, served during the French and Indian War, settled in Middleton, Connecticut, by 1775, a Loyalist soldier from 1776 until 1778, later settled in Antigonish, Nova Scotia, by 1786, memorial dated 20 May 1783, Halifax, [HMC.IV]; Lieutenant Colonel of the Prince of Wales Regiment from 1778 until 1782, then Lieutenant Colonel of the Nova Scotia Volunteers. [OBA.60] [UEL.I.131]

HOAR, CHARLES, Ensign or Volunteer of the Royal Irish Regiment around 1770. [PEF.183]

HOGAN, JAMES, born 1721 in Ireland, settled in Scotland Neck along the Roanoke River, North Carolina around 1750, was appointed Colonel of the 7th American Regiment in 1776, fought at the Battle of Germantown, Pennsylvania, was promoted to Brigadier General in 1779, was at the Siege of Charleston, South Carolina, he died at Haddrel's Point on 4 January 1781. [IS/XVII.69]

HOGAN, JOHN, from Ireland, a former soldier of the 58th [Rutlandshire] Regiment, settled in Drummond, Ontario, on 23 October 1817. [PAO.ms154]

HOGAN, MICHAEL, born 1780, enlisted in the British Army in Limerick in 1804, discharged in St John in 1818, settled in Dalhousie, Nova Scotia, in 1820. [TNA.WO.25.548]

HOGAN, TEAGE, a soldier of Lieutenant Colonel John Codrington's Company on Barbados in 1679. [H2.173]

HOLLAM, JOHN, a soldier of Lord Blakeney's Regiment, deserted in New York in 1758. [NRS.GD45.2.3.16]

HOLLAND, JAMES, a private of the Inniskilling Regiment of Dragoons, trial papers, 12 December 1808. [NRS.JC26.1808.38]

HOLLAND, JAMES, formerly a private of the Glengarry Fencibles, settled in Drummond, Ontario, on 16 July1816. [PAO.ms154]

HOLLAND, JOHN, born 1743 in Ireland, straight and well made, 5 foot six inches, a tailor, was recruited in Boston, Massachusetts, by Captain Cosnan of the 45th [Nottinghamshire] Regiment of Foot, on 2 January 1758. [NRS.GD45.2.24.4B]

HOLLAND, STEPHEN, a Captain of the Prince of Wales American Regiment during the French and Indian Wars, later Captain of a Militia Regiment in Hillsborough, New Hampshire, a Loyalist who in 1787 intended to settle in Coleraine, Ireland. [TNA.AO12.84.1]

HOLLAND, THOMAS, a Sergeant of the 18th [Royal Regiment of Ireland] Foot in Philadelphia, Pennsylvania, in 1770, in New York in 1775. [TNA.W0.76/25]

HOLLAND, WILLIAM, born 1727 in Ireland, a blacksmith in Frederick, Virginia, a soldier in Major Andrew Lewis's Company in Virginia in 1757. [VCS]

HOLMES, ..., a Captain of Lord Blakeney's Regiment, was wounded at the Siege of Ticonderoga, New York, in July 1758.

HOLMES, HUGH, a soldier of the 18th [Royal Regiment of Ireland] Foot in Philadelphia, Pennsylvania, in 1770, was promoted to Corporal on 25 October 1770, in Philadelphia. [TNA.WO.76/25]

HOLMES, SAMUEL, an army surgeon, bound from Cork to Quebec, a journal from 1814 until 1815. [PRONI.T1970]

HONAN, TEAGUE, a soldier in Captain Liston's Company on Barbados in 1679. [TNA.CO1.44.47]

HONEYMAN, JOHN, born 1729 in County Armagh, enlisted in the British Army in 1758 and sent to Canada, fought at the Sieges of Louisbourg in 1758 and at Quebec in 1759, settled in Pennsylvania in 1764, possible employed by George Washington as a spy, died in Lamington, New Jersey, on 22 August 1822.

HOPE, JOHN, Major of the 18th [Royal Regiment of Ireland] Foot, dispositions, 1826-1830. [NRS.GD253.146.10-11B]

HOPPER, THOMAS, emigrated from Ireland, a merchant in Charleston, South Carolina, joined the British forces at Lampreys Point, settled in Kingston, Jamaica, by 1783. [TNA.AO12.51.199]

HORE, Lieutenant E. G., son of Captain Hore of the Royal Navy, of Pole Hore, County Wexford, Ireland, married Maria Reid, daughter of Lieutenant Colonel Reid the Governor of the Windward Islands, in Barbados on 17 June 1847. [GM ns 28.312]

HORNER, ALEXANDER, born 1778, enlisted in the British Army in Templepatrick, County Antrim, Ireland, in 1804, discharged in St John in 1818, settled in Dalhousie, Nova Scotia, in 1820. [TNA.WO.25.548]

HOUSTON, Captain JAMES, born in Ireland, died in Iredell County, North Carolina, on 6 August 1819. [Raleigh Register, 27 August 1819]

HOWARD, FRANCIS, Ensign of the 18th [Royal Regiment of Ireland] Foot died on 29 April 1771. [TNA.WO.76/25] [PEF.185]

HOWARD, WILLIAM, a soldier of the 18th [Royal Regiment of Ireland] Foot in Charlestown Heights, Massachusetts, in 1775. [TNA.WO.12.3801]

HOWE, Lord GEORGE AUGUSTUS, an Irish peer, Colonel of the 55th [Westmoreland] Foot, a Brigadier on the American Establishment, was killed in action near Ticonderoga, New York, on 6 July 1758. [SM.20.442][IR.33]

HOWELL, THOMAS, a soldier of the 18th [Royal Regiment of Ireland] Foot in Philadelphia, Pennsylvania, in 1770, recruiting in New York in 1775. [TNA.WO.76/25]

HOYLAND, ..., a former Sergeant Major of the York Chasseurs, settled in Bathurst, Ontario, on 1 October 1819. [PAO.ms154]

HUDSON, JAMES, born 1765, enlisted in the British Army in Tipperary in 1804, discharged in St John in 1818, settled in Dalhousie, Nova Scotia, in 1820. [TNA.WO.25.548]

HUDSON, Sergeant THOMAS, of the Volunteers of Ireland Regiment fought at the Battle of Camden, South Carolina, on 16 August 1780.

HUGHES, JOHN, from Ireland, formerly a private in the 6th [Inniskilling Dragoons] Regiment, settled in Drummond, Ontario, on 31 March 1817. [PAO.ms154]

HUGHES, PATRICK, born 1734 in Ireland, a soldier who enlisted in Captain Christopher Gist's Company in Lancaster, Virginia, on 19 November 1755. [VCS]

HUMPHREYS, RICHARD, a soldier of the 28th [North Gloucestershire] Regiment of Foot, from Cork to Canada in May 1757, fought at Quebec on 13 September 1759, a journal. [BL. Blechynden Papers, vol. LXXXV, Add. Ms.45662]

HUNTER, DAVID, born in Ireland, emigrated to America in 1774, settled in Albany County, New York, a Loyalist soldier of Major Jessup's Regiment from 1779 until 1783, later in England. [UEL.II.971]

HURLEY, JEREMIAH, born 1732 in Ireland, enlisted in Captain Christopher Gist's Company in Frederick, Virginia, on 10 February 1756. [VCS]

HUSSEY, JOHN, Lieutenant Colonel of the 47th Foot, who died in North America, administration, 1760, PCC. [tna]

HUSSEY, JOHN, Second Lieutenant of the Dillon Regiment, of the Irish Brigade in French Service, in America between 1778 and 1783. [IS.XIII.51]

HUTCHISON, HUGH, born 1774, enlisted in the British Army in County Armagh in 1805, discharged in St John in 1818, settled in Dalhousie, Nova Scotia, in 1820. [TNA.WO.25.548]

INGRAM, HENRY, a soldier of the 18th [Royal Regiment of Ireland] Foot in Philadelphia, Pennsylvania, in 1767. [TNA.WO.76/25]

INSLEY, Corporal CHARLES, of the 18th [Royal Regiment of Ireland] Foot in 1767, a Corporal of the regiment in Philadelphia, Pennsylvania, in 1767.   [TNA.WO.76/25] [PEF.15]

IRISH, JAMES, of the Royal Irish Artillery, was discharged in 1767. [TNA.WO.97.1238.50]

IRVINE, WILLIAM, born 3 November 1741 in County Fermanagh, a Cornet of Dragoons, then a ship's surgeon, served during the French and Indian War/the Seven Year War from 1756 until 1763, then settled in Pennsylvania, in 1776 as Colonel of the Pennsylvania Regiment took part in an unsuccessful attack on Canada, in 1779 he was a Brigadier General of the Continental Army until 1783, he died in Philadelphia, Pennsylvania, on 29 July 1804.

IRWIN, ALEXANDER BURROWES, late of the 32nd [Cornwall] Regiment, then a planter on St Vincent, died on 22 July 1806. [St Vincent gravestone]

IRWIN, JAMES, late of the 97th [Royal Ulster Regiment] Foot, settled in Bathurst, Ontario, on 7 October 1819. [PAO.ms154]

IRWIN, JOHN R., an Ensign in the West Indies, a journal from 1808 until 1813. [PRONI.DOD.1515.1]

ISAAC WILLIAM, born 1700 in County Cavan, a weaver, later a Sergeant of the 35th [Royal Sussex] Regiment of Foot at Fort Edward, New York, in 1757. [TNA.WO.116.5.20]

IVORY, THOMAS, a soldier stationed at Placentia, Newfoundland, in 1732. [TNA.CO194.24.109]

JAMESON, ALEXANDER, a Lieutenant of O'Farrel's Regiment of Foot, 'sailed round the world with Commander Anson', was killed in a duel in Dublin on 28 September 1754. [SM.16.500]

JENNICK WILLIAM, a Lieutenant of the 27th [Inniskilling] Regiment, at Fort George, New York, on 4 September 1757. [NRS.GD45.2.35.2]

JENNINGS, JOHN, from Ireland, late of the Royal Artillery, settled in Beckwith, Ontario, on 28 March 1818. [PAO.ms154]

JOHNSON, ANDREW, born 1728 in Ireland, a linen draper in Norfolk County, Virginia, enlisted in the Virginia Regiment on 19 May 1756. [VCS]

JOHNSON, GUY, born in Ireland, emigrated to America in 1755, a Captain of the Provincial Regiment of New York during the French and Indian Wars, later a Lieutenant of the British Army there, settled at Schenectady, New York, a Loyalist who moved to Canada. [TNA.AO12.22.22]; died in England on 5 March 1788.

JOHNSON, JAMES, born in Ireland, settled in Artillery Patent, Charlotte County, New York, a Loyalist soldier in 1777, moved to Mashishe, Canada. [OBA.915]

JOHNSON, JOHN, born 1718 in Dublin, 5 foot 10 inches tall, deserted from Captain Robert Hodgson's Independent Company in 1746. [VaGaz.27.6.1746]

JOHNSON, JOHN, late of the Glengarry Fencibles, settled in Bathurst, Ontario, on 23 July 1816. [PAO.ms154]

JOHNSON, THOMAS, a soldier of the 18th [Royal Regiment of Ireland] Foot in Philadelphia, Pennsylvania, in 1767. [TNA.WO.76/25]

JOHNSON, Sir WILLIAM, born 1715 in Smithtown, County Meath, settled in the Mohawk Valley, New York, in 1738, fought during the French and India War notably at Crown Point and at Lake George, later at Niagara in 1759 and the Siege of Montreal, Quebec, in 1760, he died on 11 July 1774. [GM.46.446, etc]

JOHNSTON, GEORGE, an Ensign of the Inniskilling Regiment of Foot in 1691, a Lieutenant of Colonel Gustavus Hamilton's Regiment of Foot on 24 March 1692, was appointed 1st Lieutenant of Colonel Luke Lillington's Regiment of Foot 'designed for Jamaica' on 24 December 1694. [DAL.III.206/263]

JOHNSTON, THOMAS, of 5 Brown Street, Belfast, late of the 1st [Royal Scots] Foot, applied to settle in Canada on 26 May 1827. [TNA.CO384.16]

JONES, GEORGE, from Ireland, formerly a private of the 4th Royal Veteran Battalion, settled in Burgess, Ontario, on 30 June 1817. [PAO.ms154]

JONES, JOHN, late of the Royal Sappers, settled in Lanark, Ontario, on 1 November 1820. [PAO.ms154]

JORDAN, JOHN, born in Ireland, settled in Morris County, New Jersey, recruited me for the British Army, a Captain in British service, moved to the Bahamas in 1784. [TNA.AO12102.194]

KEARNEY, JAMES, a soldier of the 2nd Battalion of the 84th [Royal Highland Emigrants Regiment] Foot, aboard the frigate Raleigh bound from New York to Charleston, South Carolina, in 1780. [NRS.GD174.2405]

KEARNS, THOMAS, a former Corporal of the Royal Artillery, settled in Bathurst, Ontario, on 24 July 1817. [PAO.ms154]

KEATING, JOHN, a Second Lieutenant of the Walsh Regiment, of the Irish Brigade in French Service, in America between 1778 and 1783. [IS.XIII.51]

KEATING, WILLIAM, a Lieutenant of the Walsh Regiment, of the Irish Brigade in French Service, in America between 1778 and 1783. [IS.XIII.51]

KEHOE, JAMES, from Ireland, a former private of the 49th [Hertfordshire] Regiment, settled in Bathurst, Ontario, on 12 August 1817. [PAO.ms154]

KEATON, MICHAEL, born in Ireland, formerly an officer of the British Light Horse, was sought for seizing a ship on 2 October 1784. [PaGaz.2837]

KEGAN, THOMAS, born 1731 in Ireland, a farmer in Augusta, Virginia, a soldier in Major Andrew Lewis's Company in Virginia in 1757. [VCS]

KELLY, E., Quartermaster of the King's Own Regiment, died in the West Indies in 182-. [St Michael's Cathedral tablet, Bridgetown, Barbados]

KELLY, FRANCIS JOHN, Lieutenant of the 18th [Royal Regiment of Ireland] Foot around 1770. [PEF.169]; was promoted to be Captain-Lieutenant of the same regiment in place of John Peter de Lancey, on 29 July 1780. [SM.42.391]

KELLY, HUGH, raised troops in Maryland, Virginia and Pennsylvania, for the British, entitled the Maryland Royal Retaliators, he was sought by the rebels with a £500 reward offered, but escaped to New York. [HMC.American.iii.46]

KELLY, JAMES, a soldier of Captain Harrison's Company on Barbados in 1679. [TNA.CO1.44.47]

KELLY, JOHN, a Sergeant of Captain Tim Thornhill's Company of Militia on Barbados in 1679. [TNA.CO1.44.47] [H2.80]

KELLY, LAWRENCE, born 1727 in Ireland, a mason in Brunswick County, Virginia, a soldier in Major Andrew Lewis's Company in Virginia in 1757. [VCS]

KELLY, MARK, a soldier of Captain Harrison's Company on Barbados in 1679. [TNA.CO1.44.47]

KELLY, MATTHEW, a soldier stationed at Placentia, Newfoundland, in 1732. [TNA.CO194.24.109]

KELLY, PATRICK, from Ireland, a former private of the Glengarry Regiment, settled in Drummond, Ontario, on 16 July 1816. [PAO.ms154]

KELLY, PETER, from Ireland, a former private of the 43rd [Monmouthshire Regiment] Foot, settled in Burgess, Ontario, on 9 August 1817. [PAO.ms154]

KELLY, PHILLIP, a soldier of Captain Harrison's Company on Barbados in 1679. [TNA.CO1.44.47]

KELLY, ROBERT, a soldier or militiaman in Colonel Lyne's Regiment of Foot in Barbados on 6 January 1679. [H2.112]

KELLY, THOMAS, from Ireland, a former soldier of the York Chasseurs, settled in Bathurst, Ontario, on 2 September 1819. [PAO.ms154]

KELLEY, THOMAS, born 1768, enlisted in the British Army in County Clare in 1804, discharged in St John in 1818, settled in Dalhousie, Nova Scotia, in 1820. [TNA.WO.25.548]

KELLY, WILLIAM, a soldier of Captain Thornhill's Company on Barbados in 1679. [TNA.CO1.44.47] [HS.80]

KELSEY, JOHN, born 1733 in Ireland, a tailor in Winchester, Virginia, a soldier of Captain Henry Woodward's Company in Virginia, on 11 September 1757. [VCS]

KELTING, JOHN, born 1732 in Ireland, a labourer who was recruited into Stewart's Light Horse in Virginia on 17 May 1756. [VCS]

KENDALL, OLIVER S., born 1721, 'fought under Admiral Rodney in his engagement with De Grasse, also circumnavigated the globe three times', died at Warrenpoint, Ireland, on 8 September 1823. [SM.92.512]

KENNEDY, JOHN, a Sergeant stationed at Placentia, Newfoundland, in 1732. [TNA.CO194.24.109]

KENNEDY, Dr MATTHEW, from Ireland to America in 1772, settled at Stow Creek, Cumberland County, New Jersey, a Captain of the Loyal American Rangers until 1783, he returned to Ireland and died in London around 1784. [TNA.AO12.17.152]

KENT, JAMES, from Ireland, formerly a private of the 6th [Inniskilling Dragoons] Regiment, settled in Beckwith, Ontario, on 6 April 1818. [PAO.ms154]

KEOGH, MYLES WALTER, born 1840, an army officer in America, letters from 1861 until 1869, to his brother Thomas Keogh in County Carlow, Ireland. [NLI.ms3885]

KERBY, THOMAS NORBURY, Commander-in-Chief of Antigua and Montserrat, died in Antigua in November 1819. [F.J.4.2.1820]

KERRINGTON, THOMAS, late of the Glengarry Fencibles, settled in Bathurst, Ontario, on 23 July 1816. [PAO.ms154]

KERRY, MICHAEL, born in Ireland, served in the British Army for 22 years, settled on Cape Breton, Nova Scotia, around 1799, petitioned for a land grant on the Sydney River, N.S., in 1809. [NSARM.mf15790]

KERWEN, JOSEPH, a Lieutenant of the Militia on Montserrat in 1705. [SPAWI.1705.1347i]

KIDNEY, JAMES, from Ireland, late of the Royal Sappers, settled in Lanark, Ontario, on 1 November 1820. [PAO.ms154]

KING, GILBERT, an Ensign in Montreal and Niagara in Canada also Crown Point and Fort William Henry in New York, a notebook from 1761 until 1768 [NLI.ms3240]

KING, JAMES, a soldier of the 18th [Royal Regiment of Ireland] Foot in Philadelphia, Pennsylvania, in 1767. [TNA.WO.76/25]

KINNEAR, DAVID, formerly a Lieutenant of the Royal Artillery, settled in Bathurst, Ontario, on 1 April 1820. [PAO.ms154]

KINNIN, [or Kinyon], GEORGE, a soldier of the 18th [Royal Regiment of Ireland] Foot in Philadelphia, Pennsylvania, in 1767, at Charleston Heights, Massachusetts, in 1775. [TNA.WO.76/25][TNA.WO12.3501]

KNIGHT, JOHN, a soldier of the 18th [Royal Regiment of Ireland] Foot in Philadelphia, Pennsylvania, in 1767; was killed in Illinois in March 1772. [PEF.15] [TNA.WO.76/25]

KNOTT, DANIEL, late of the Royal Sappers, settled in Lanark, Ontario, on 1 November 1820. [PAO.ms154]

KNOWLES, Lieutenant WILLIAM, in Montserrat in 1677. [TNA]

KNOX, Cornet JAMES, died aged 88, 'he was at the raising of the Royal Irish Dragoons, served in nineteen campaigns in King William's and Queen Anne's wars', 1752. [SM.15.628]

LACEY, MAURICE, a soldier of Captain Hall's Company on Barbados in 1679. [TNA.CO1.44.47]

LAMB, JOHN, from Ireland, a former Sergeant of the 4th Royal Veteran Battalion, settled in Young, Ontario, on 31 July 1817. [PAO.ms154]

LAMBERT, JOSEPH, a soldier of the 18TH [Royal Regiment of Ireland] Foot in Philadelphia, Pennsylvania, in 1770, enlisted on 24 June 1770 and deserted [?] on 20 August 1770. [TNA.WO.76/25]

LANE, DENNIS, late of the Royal Sappers, settled in Lanark, Ontario, on 1 November 1820. [PAO.ms154]

LANE, JOHN, emigrated from Ireland to America, settled in Schenectady, New York, by 1760, a Loyalist soldier who moved to Hope Town, Chaleur Bay, Canada, by 1787. [OBA.231]

LANE, MATTHEW, Captain or Captain Lieutenant of the 18th [Royal Regiment of Ireland] Foot around 1770. [PEF.121]

LATIMER, HARRY, late Sergeant of the Royal Artillery, settled in Burgess, Ontario, on 26 October 1819. [PAO.ms154]

LATIMER, HUGH, from Ireland, formerly a Sergeant of the Royal Artillery, settled in Burgess, Ontario, on 26 December 1817. [PAO.ms154]

LATTIN, PATRICK, born 1726 in Ireland, a planter who enlisted in Captain William Bronaugh's Company, in Frederick, Virginia, in December 1755. [VCS]

LAWRENCE, JOHN, emigrated from Ireland to America in 1766, settled in Camden, Charlotte County, New York, a Loyalist soldier from 1776, later in Oswegatchie. [UEL.II.1087]

LAWRENCE, JOHN, emigrated from Ireland to America in 1766, settled in Johnstown, Tryon County, New York, a Loyalist in the 1st Battalion of Sir John Johnson's Regiment [Royal Regiment of New York] from 1778 until 1783, moved to New Johnstown, Ontario, by 1783. [UEL.II.1121]

LEAHY, WILLIAM, born in Ireland, a trader in Haverstraw, Orange County, New York, served as an NCO of the 1st New York Regiment during the Revolutionary War, a Loyalist claim in 1788. [TNA.AO12.31.151]

LEAN, JOSEPH, late private of the Glengarry Regiment, settled in Drummond, Ontario, on 18 July 1816. [PAO.ms154]

LEAREY, JOHN, born 1782, late of the 16th [Princess Victoria's] Foot, applied to settle in Canada on 12 June 1827. [TNA.CO384.16]

LEATHES, STANLEY, Staff Officer of the 18th [Royal Regiment of Ireland] Foot. around 1770. [PEF.208]

LEE, JOHN, from Ireland, a former soldier of the 2nd Battalion of the 89th [Princess Victoria's] Regiment, settled in Bathurst, Ontario, on 9 August 1817. [PAO.ms154]

LEE, PETER, born 1660 in Dublin, Ireland, lived in England, a soldier in Flanders, died in Antigua on 8 October 1704. [St John's Cathedral, Antigua]

LEE, SAMUEL, a soldier of the 18th [Royal Regiment of Ireland] Foot in Philadelphia, Pennsylvania, in 1767, at Charleston Heights, Massachusetts, missing in 1775. [TNA.WO.76/25; TNA.WO12.3501]

LEE, SAMUEL, master tailor of the 18th [Royal Regiment of Ireland] Foot, was captured at Lexington, Massachusetts, in 1775. [TNA.WO.76/25]

LEONARD, JAMES, a former Sergeant of the Royal Sappers, settled in Lanark, Ontario, on 1 November 1820. [PAO.ms154]

LET, ..., a Captain of the 26th Regiment, emigrated via Waterford aboard the Lynx bound for Quebec, landed there on 17 May 1820. [QM]

LEWIS, ANDREW, born 9 October 1720 in County Donegal, settled in Pennsylvania and later in Augusta County, Virginia, an officer of the Virginia Regiment, fought in the French and Indian War under George Washington at the capture of Fort Necessity, he died in Bedford, Virginia, on 26 September 1781. [VCS]

LIDDEL, ANDREW, emigrated from Ireland to America, settled in Schenectady, New York, before 1776, a Loyalist soldier under General Burgoyne, moved to Caldwell's Manor, Quebec, by 1783. [UEL.II.1206]

LIGHTWOOD, WILLIAM, a soldier of the 18th [Royal Regiment of Ireland] Foot, in Philadelphia, Pennsylvania, in 1770, deserted on 24 August 1770. [TNA.WO.76/25]

LINDSEY, ALEXANDER, a soldier of the 18th [Royal Regiment of Ireland] Foot, at Charleston Heights, Massachusetts, in 1775. [TNA.WO12.3501]

LINDSAY, DAVID, from Rathfriland, County Down, a soldier in Barbados, letters between 1804 and 1808. [PRONI.DOD.687]

LINEN, ANDREW, emigrated from Ireland to Boston, Massachusetts in 1763, a shopkeeper, a Loyalist soldier who settled in Nova Scotia in 1783. [TNA.AO12.10.90]

LINN, JOHN, Surgeon's mate, of the 18th [Royal Regiment of Ireland] Foot, in Illinois in 1774. [TNA.WO.76/25]

LINN, WILLIAM, born 1731 in Ireland, a carpenter who was recruited into Stewart's Light Horse in Virginia on 24 December 1755. [VCS]

LINNAN, JAMES, a soldier of the 18th [Royal Regiment of Ireland] Foot in Philadelphia, Pennsylvania, in 1767. [TNA.WO.76/25]

LLOYD, MICHAEL, born in Ireland, settled in Philadelphia, Pennsylvania, joined the British forces in 1777, served in the 52nd [Oxfordshire] Regiment later in the 57th Regiment, moved to Cumberland, Upper Canada, by 1786. [PAO.LC.657]

LLOYD, WILLIAM, born in Ireland, emigrated from Ireland to America in 1771, a distiller in Baltimore, Maryland, until 1776, a soldier of the 85th Regiment, returned to Ireland, settled in Ballymore, County Meath, in 1786. [TNA.AO126.148]

LOGAN, COLLOE, born 1726 in Ireland, a weaver, enlisted in Captain Christopher Gist's Company in Lancaster, Pennsylvania, on 19 November 1755, a soldier in Captain Robert Spotswood's Company at Fort Young in 1757. [VCS]

LOGAN, JOHN, a soldier of the 18th [Royal Regiment of Ireland] Foot in Philadelphia, Pennsylvania, in 1767; at Charleston Heights, Massachusetts, in 1775. [TNA.WO.76/25; WO12.3501]

LONERGAN, MICHAEL, born 1776, enlisted in the British Army in Cork in 1805, was discharged in St John in 1818, settled in Dalhousie, Nova Scotia, in 1820. [TNA.WO.25.548]

LONERGAN, WILLIAM, born 1773, enlisted in the British Army in Cork in 1805, was discharged in St John in 1818, settled in Dalhousie, Nova Scotia, in 1820. [TNA.WO.25.548]

LONERGAN, WILLIAM, born 1779, enlisted in the British Army in Cashel, County Tipperary, in 1804, was discharged in Fredericton, New Brunswick, in 1818, settled in Dalhousie, Nova Scotia, in 1820. [TNA.WO.25.548]

LONG, JAMES, born 1776, enlisted in the British Army in Cashel, Tipperary, in 1804, was discharged in Newfoundland in 1818, settled in Dalhousie, Nova Scotia, in 1820. [TNA.WO.25.548]

LORD, HUGH, Captain or Captain Lieutenant of the 18th [Royal Regiment of Ireland] Foot, at Fort Chartres, Illinois, in 1772. [TNA.WO.76/25] [PEF.15/122]

LOUGHLAND, DENIS, soldier of Captain Samuel Woodward's Company of Militia in Barbados on 8 January 1679. [H2.156]

LOVETT, THOMAS, from Belfast and Virginia, died aboard HMS Falkland probate, 1709, PCC. [TNA]

LUCAS, ROBERT, born 1723 in Armagh, a soldier of the 27th [Inniskilling] Foot, fought in New York around 1759 during the French and Indian Wars. [TNA.WO.120.4]

LUND, JOHN, a soldier of the 18th [Royal Regiment of Ireland] Foot in Philadelphia, Pennsylvania, in 1767. [TNA.WO.76/25]

LYLE, MATTHEW, settled in St George's parish, Georgia, a Captain of Militia in Georgia, later with the Corps of Rangers in East Florida, finally Lieutenant Colonel of Militia in Georgia, moved to Larne, Ireland, by 1785. [TNA.AO12.101.121]

LYNCH, DISNEY, deserted the 60th Regiment in New York, later court martialled at Fort George, New York, in 1757. [TNA.WO.71.66]

LYNCH, ISODORE, Second Captain of the Dillon Regiment, of the Irish Brigade in French Service, in America between 1778 and 1783. [IS.XIII.51]

LYNCH, JAMES, born 1730 in Ireland, enlisted in Captain Christopher Gist's Company in Baltimore, Maryland, on 23 February 1756. [VCS]

LYNCH, JAMES, born 1730 in Ireland, a militiaman who absconded from the Virginia Regiment in 1756. [VaGaz.294]

LYNCH, MATTHEW, born 1731 in Ireland, a planter who was recruited for William Cox's Rangers in Virginia On 26 September 1755. [VCS]

LYNCH, SAMUEL SMITH, a Lieutenant of the 1st West Indian Regiment, in Barbados, married Catherine Rebecca Cox in Demerara in February 1824. [The Barbadian]

LYNCH, THOMAS, settled as a merchant in New York by 1757, joined the Army in July 1776, and his two sons joined the 22nd [Cheshire] Regiment, settled in Lonberry near Castlerea, Ireland, by 1789. [TNA.AO12.30.306; WO.17.124]]

LYNN, JOHN L., Staff Officer of the 18th [Royal Regiment of Ireland] Foot, a surgeon's mate in Illinois in 1775. [TNA.WO.76/25][PEF.208]

MCALISTER, MOSES, from Ireland, a former private of the 104th [North British] Regiment, settled in Bathurst, Ontario, on 30 June 1817. [PAO.ms154]

MCALISTER, SAMUEL, born in Ireland, settled as a farmer in Ninety-Six District, South Carolina, in 1774, served in the Loyalist South Carolina Militia, moved to Rawdon Township, Hants County, Nova Scotia, by 1785. [TNA.AO12.49.233][UEL.I.702]

MCALISTER, TERENCE, emigrated from Ireland to America in 1771, a farmer in Kortwright township, New York, by 1774, a Loyalist soldier in Sir John Johnson's Regiment, [the King's Royal Regiment of New York], from 1777 until 1784, settled in Sydney, Cape Breton, Nova Scotia, by 1786. [OBA.31][UEL.I.85]

MCALLEN, JAMES, a soldier of the 18th [Royal Regiment of Ireland] Foot in Charleston Heights, Massachusetts, died on 10 July 1775. [TNA.WO.12.3501]

MCCADDEN, HENRY, from Ireland, late gunner of the King's Artillery, settled in Drummond, Ontario, on 21 November 1816. [PAO.ms154]

MCCAFFERY, THOMAS, from Ireland, a former private of the 70th [Surrey] Regiment, settled in Drummond, Ontario, on 31 March 1817. [PAO.ms154]

MCCAFFREY, JOHN, emigrated from Ireland to America around 1747, settled on Sir William Johnson's land in Tryon County, New York, a Loyalist soldier from 1777 until 1783, settled in Canada. [UEL.II.1079]

MCCANE, BERNARD, late of the Royal Cork Rangers, applied to settled in Canada on 27 May 1827. [TNA.CO384.16]

MCCANN, JOHN, late of the Royal Sappers, settled in Lanark, Ontario, on 1 November 1820. [PAO.ms154]

MCCARMICK, WILLIAM, a soldier of Lord Blakeney's Regiment, deserted in New York in 1758. [NRS.GD45.2.3.16]

MCCARTHY, DANIEL, from Ireland, formerly a Sergeant of the 97th Regiment, settled in Wogard, Ontario, on 31 July 1817, later in Kittley, Ontario, on 22 May 1818. [PAO.ms154]

MACCARTHY, EWAN, a Second Lieutenant of the Walsh Regiment, of the Irish Brigade in French Service, in America between 1778 and 1783. [IS.XIII.51]

MCCARTHY, WILLIAM, from Ireland, late private of the 97th Regiment, settled in Beckwith, Ontario, on 23 July 1818. [PAO.ms154]

MACCARTY, ..., a French Army officer with 32 years of service in Louisiana by 1763. [Archive des Colonies, serie D, troupes colonials, registres D2C.50/58]

MCCLELLAND, ROBERT, emigrated from Ireland to America in 1767, settled in Craven County, South Carolina, during the American War he was a Lieutenant of the South Carolina Rangers, moved to Upper Canada [Ontario] by 1784. [PAO.LC.1148]

MCCLUSKY, ARTHUR, settled in Reading township, Little York County, Pennsylvania, before 1776, a Loyalist soldier of the Queen's Rangers, moved to Londonderry, Ireland, by 1786. [TNA.AO12.100.339]

MCCONNELL, MICHAEL, late of the York Chasseurs, settled in Bathurst, Ontario, on 22 September 1818. [PAO.ms154]

MCCONNELLY, BERNARD, born 1777, enlisted in the British Army in Louth in 1805, discharged in St John, New Brunswick, in 1818, settled in Dalhousie, Canada, in 1820. [TNA.WO.25.548]

MCCOLLOUGH, JAMES, sr., settled in Hackensack, New Jersey, from 1765 until 1776, a Militia Lieutenant of New York until 1783, settled in Ireland by 1788. [TNA.AO12.13.384]

MCCORMACK, HUGH, a soldier of the 18th [Royal Regiment of Ireland] Foot in Philadelphia, Pennsylvania, in 1767, at Charleston Heights, South Carolina, in 1775.   [TNA.WO.76/25; WO.12.3501]

MCCOURT, THOMAS, late of the Royal Sappers, settled in Lanark, Ontario, on 1 November 1820. [PAO.ms154]

MCCOY, JOHN, born 1728 in Ireland, a cooper in Norfolk, Virginia, enlisted in Captain David Bell's Company in Virginia on 18 May 1756. [VCS]

MCCRACKIN, WILLIAM, a soldier of the 18th [Royal Regiment of Ireland] Foot in Philadelphia, Pennsylvania, in 1767. [TNA.WO.76/25]

MCCULLOUGH, JAMES, settled in Camden District, South Carolina, before 1776, Captain of the Camden Militia, later moved to Belfast, Ireland, by 1783. [TNA.AO12.46234]

MCCULLOCH, JOHN, born 1716 in Northern Ireland, settled in America, Provincial officer under Rogers, Commissary of Stores at Oswego in 1756, died in London on 27 December 1793. [GM.64.89]

MCCUNING, DENIS, a militiaman of Captain Tim Thornhill's in Barbados in 1679. [TNA.CO1.44.47] [H2.80]

MCDEAD, RICHARD, to America with the 18th [Royal Regiment of Ireland] Foot in 1767, returned to Britain in 1786, discharged in 1788. [P.12]

MACDEMAROE, SHEDA, a soldier of Captain Hall's Company on Barbados in 1679. [TNA.CO1.44.47]

MACDERMOTT, BERNARD, Lieutenant of the Dillon Regiment, of the Irish Brigade in French Service, in America between 1778 and 1783. [IS.XIII.51]

MACDERMOTT, THOMAS, [1], Second Captain of the Dillon Regiment, of the Irish Brigade in French Service, in America between 1778 and 1783. [IS.XIII.51]

MACDERMOTT, THOMAS, [2], Second Captain of the Dillon Regiment, of the Irish Brigade in French Service, in America between 1778 and 1783. [IS.XIII.51]

MCDONALD, JOHN, born 1714 in Ireland, a barber in Norfolk County, Virginia, enlisted in the Virginia Regiment on 19 May 1756. [VCS]

MACDONALD, JOHN BAPTISTE, Sub Lieutenant of the Dillon Regiment, of the Irish Brigade in French Service, in America between 1778 and 1783. [IS.XIII.51]

MCDONALD, ROBERT, born 1731 in Dublin, Ireland, enlisted in Captain Christopher Gist's Company in Lancaster, Pennsylvania, on 14 November 1755. [VCS]

MCDONALD, TERANCE, born 1734 in Ireland, a planter in Amelia, Virginia, a soldier of Captain Henry Woodward's Company in Virginia, on 11 September 1757. [VCS]

MCDONNELL, JOSEPH, participated in the Rebellion of 1798, settled in USA by 1812. [TNA.I.999/49]

MACDONEL, RANDEL, emigrated from Ireland to America, settled on the Mohawk River, Tryon County, New York, he and his four sons joined the British Army at Fort Stanwix in 1777, he was a Sergeant of Butler's Rangers, moved to Niagara, Ontario, by 1783. [OBA.284]

MCELROY, JOHN, a soldier of the 18th [Royal Regiment of Ireland] Foot in Philadelphia, Pennsylvania, in 1767; in Charleston Heights, Massachusetts, deserted on 25 July 1775. [TNA.WO.76/25; TNA.WO12.3501]

MCELROY, ROBERT, born 1714 in Ireland, a sawyer from Orange County, Virginia, a soldier in Captain Robert Spotswood's Company at Fort Young in 1757. [VCS]

MCEWAN, ARCHIBALD, a soldier of the 18th [Royal Regiment of Ireland] Foot in Philadelphia, Pennsylvania, in 1767, in Charleston Heights, South Massachusetts, in 1775. [TNA.WO.76/25; WO.12.3501]

MCFARLAND, WILLIAM, in Portsmouth, Virginia, a letter to his father John McFarland in Philadelphia, Pennsylvania, describing his time as a Union soldier at the Siege of Richmond, Virginia, in 1864. [PRONI.D732]

MCFARRELL, JAMES, in 5 Brown Street, Belfast, late of the 50th [Queen's Own] Foot, applied to settle in Canada on 26 May 1827. [TNA.CO384.16]

MCGEE, ALEXANDER, I 22 Union Street, Belfast, formerly a private of the 47th Foot, applied to settle in Canada in April 1827. [TNA.CO384.16]

MCGEE, HENRY, emigrated from Ireland to America in 1773, settled in Chambers Town and later in Perth Valley, Cumberland County, Pennsylvania, a Loyalist and a British soldier, moved to Nova Scotia in 1778, settled at Wilmot by 1786. [UEL.I.537]

MCGENNETT, DAVID, born 1717 in Ireland, a sawyer in Loudoun, Virginia, enlisted in March 1756, a soldier in Colonel George Washington's Company in 1757. [VCS]

MCGIE, JOHN, a soldier of Lord Blakeney's Regiment, deserted in New York in 1758. [NRS.GD45.2.3.16]

MCGILL, JAMES, born 1784, enlisted in the British Army in County Cavan in 1805, discharged in 1818, settled in Dalhousie, Nova Scotia, in 1820. [TNA.WO25.548]

MCGILL, ROBERT, born 1795, enlisted in the British Army in County Tyrone in 1813, discharged in St John in 1818, settled in Dalhousie, Nova Scotia, in 1820. [TNA.WO25.548]

MCGINNIS, JOHN, from Ireland, formerly a Sergeant of the Glengarry Fencibles, settled in Drummond, Ontario, on 16 July 1816. [PAO.ms154]

MCGINNIS, WILLIAM, from Ireland, formerly a private of the Glengarry Fencibles, settled in Drummond, Ontario, on 16 July 1816. [PAO.ms154]

MCGLAUGHLAN, WILLIAM, emigrated from Ireland to America in 1773, settled in Cherry Valley, Tryon County, New York, a Loyalist soldier in Sir John Johnson's Regiment, [the King's Royal Regiment of New York], from 1776 until 1783, then moved to New Johnstown, Canada. [UEL.II.1182]

MCGOWAN, THOMAS, born 1778, enlisted in the British Army in County Armagh in 1805, discharged in St John in 1818, settled in Dalhousie, Nova Scotia, in 1820. [TNA.WO25.548]

MCGRAH, DENIS, a militiaman in Captain William Allanby's Company on Barbados in 1679. [H2.70

MCGRAGH, GARRETT, probably from Cork, settled in Middletown, Connecticut, from 1765 to 1774, a Loyalist Lieutenant, returned to Cork. [TNA.12.104.43]

MCGRATH, TERENCE, a soldier of the 2nd Battalion of the 84th [Royal Emigrants Regiment] Foot, aboard the frigate Raleigh bound from New York to Charleston, South Carolina, in 1780. [NRS.GD174.2405]

MCGAUGH, WILLIAM, born 1727 in Ireland, a planter in Frederick, Virginia, enlisted in August 1756, a soldier of Colonel George Washington's Company in August 1757. [VCS]

MCGRAW, THOMAS, born in Ireland, a former marine, absconded from John Van Sart in Kent County, Maryland, on 10 July 1769. [PaGaz.2117]

MCGUIGAN, JOHN, late of the Royal Sappers, settled in Lanark, Ontario, on 1 November 1820. [PAO.ms154]

MCGUIRE, JOHN, from Ireland, late a private of the 17th Light Dragoons, settled in Drummond, Ontario, on 17 October 1816. [PAO.ms154]

MCGUIRE, PHILIP, Second Captain of the Dillon Regiment, of the Irish Brigade in French Service, in America between 1778 and 1783. [IS.XIII.51]

MCHEWAN, ROBERT, from Ireland, formerly of the 4th Royal Veterans, settled in Elmsby, Ontario, on 27 February 1818. [PAO.ms154]

MCILMOYLE, JAMES, emigrated from Ireland to America, settled in New York before 1776, a Loyalist soldier from 1777, settled in Montreal, Quebec, by 1783. [PAO.LC783]

MACKANALLY ,....., son of Hugh Mackanally of Anaghmackmanis, near Charlemont, County Armagh, a soldier in Captain Stewart's Company of the 4th Battalion of the 'English train, [in America?],a letter dated Anaghmackmanis 1 January 1783. [HMC. American, iii.312]

MCKEAN, JAMES, from Ireland, a former private of the Glengarry Regiment, settled in Drummond, Ontario, on 16 July 1816. [PAO.ms154]

MCKENNEDY, NEAL, a soldier of Captain Samuel Woodward's Company of Militia in Barbados on 8 January 1679. [H2.156]

MCKENZIE, LAWRENCE, a soldier of Lord Blakeney's Regiment, deserted in New York in 1758. [NRS.GD45.2.3.16]

MCKENZIE, LAWRENCE, emigrated from Ireland to America in 1752, settled in Skenesborough, New York, a Loyal soldier in Roger's Rangers, moved to Carlisle, Nova Scotia. [UEL.I.330]

MCKETRICK, MICHAEL, late of the Royal Sappers, settled in Lanark, Ontario, on 1 November 1820. [PAO.ms154]

MCKIBBEN, HENRY, probably from Portaferry, County Down, a naval surgeon in Halifax, Nova Scotia, by 1813. [PRONI.T3103/1]

MACKIM, JAMES, born in Ireland, emigrated to America in 1774, settled in Albany County, New York, a Loyalist soldier from 1776 until 1783, moved to Sorel, Quebec. [UEL.II.918]

MCKRICKETT, DANIEL, a soldier of Captain Samuel Woodward's Company of Militia in Barbados on 8 January 1679. [H2.156]

MCLAIN, PATRICK, born 1733 in Ireland, a planter in Augusta, Virginia, enlisted in September 1756, a soldier of Colonel George Washington's Company in August 1757. [VCS]

MCLAINEY, PATRICK, in Granard, County Longford, late of the 32nd [Cornwall] Regiment, applied to settle in Canada on 20 March 1827. [TNA.CO384.16]

MCLEAN, JAMES, a Sergeant of the Glengarry Fencibles, settled in Wolford, Ontario, on 25 October 1819. [PAO.ms154]

MCLEAN, JOHN, born 1665, 'a drummer in King William's army in Ireland' died in Orange County, New York, in August 1770. [SM.32.630]

MACLELLAN, WILLIAM, emigrated from Ireland to America in 1768, settled in Cherry Valley, New York, joined Colonel Butler's Rangers in 1779 and served throughout the war, at Mashishi, Ontario, or Quebec by 1783. [OBA][UEL.II.996]

MCLELLAND, ROBERT, emigrated from Ireland to America in 1767, settled in Craven County, South Carolina, a Loyalist and a Lieutenant of the South Carolina Rangers. [UEL.II.1148]

MACLOSKY, JAMES, Sub Lieutenant of the Dillon Regiment, of the Irish Brigade in French Service, in America between 1778 and 1783. [IS.XIII.51]

MCMAHON, FRANCIS, born 1791, enlisted in the British Army in Dublin in 1811, discharged from the 8th Regiment in St John's, Newfoundland, in 1818, settled in Dalhousie, Nova Scotia, in 1820. [TNA.WO.25.548]

MCMAHON, HUGH, a private of the Glengarry Fencibles, settled in Wolford, Ontario, on 16 July 1816. [PAO.ms154]

MCMAHON, MICHAEL, in Dunmanway, late of the 18th Dragoons, applied to settle in Canada on 8 February 1827. [TNA.CO384.16]

MCMAHON, MICHAEL, born 1777, in Dunmanway, late of the 18th Hussars, applied to settle in Canada on 12 June 1827. [TNA.CO384.16]

MCMANUS, JOHN, a private of the 27th [Inniskilling] Regiment, trial papers, 18 April 1814. [NRS.JC26.1814.22]

MCMANUS, JOHN, in 5 Brown Street, Belfast, late of the 12th Veteran Battalion, applied to settle in Canada on 26 May 1827. [TNA.CO384.16]

MCMARTH, WILLIAM, born 1724 in Ireland, a weaver in Baltimore, a soldier of Captain Robert Spotswood's Company in Fort Young, Virginia, on 4 October 1757. [VCS]

MCMATH, WILLIAM, born 1716 in Ireland, enlisted in Captain Christopher Gist's Company in Baltimore, Maryland, on 15 February 1756. [VCS]

MCMORRIS, ALEXANDER, a soldier of the 18th [Royal Regiment of Ireland] Foot, in New York in 1775. [TNA.WO.76/25]

MCMULLEN, JAMES, a soldier of the 18th [Royal Regiment of Ireland] Foot, in Philadelphia, Pennsylvania, in 1772. [TNA.WO.76/25]

MACMURROW, JOHN, a militiaman in Barbados in 1679. [TNA.CO1.44.47]

MACMURROW, TEAGE, a militiaman in Barbados in 1679. [TNA.CO1.44.47]

MCNALLY, RICHARD, of the Royal Garrison Battalion, deceased, a memorial by his widow Esther McNally dated 1782. [HMC.American.iii.304]

MCNAMARA, DENIS, born 1730 in Ireland, a planter who was recruited for William Cox's Rangers in Virginia On 21 October 1755. [VCS]

MCNEAL, HUGH, emigrated from Ireland to America in 1763, a farmer in Bedford County, Pennsylvania, by 1775, a Loyalist soldier from 1777 until 1783, settled in Burton, St John, New Brunswick, by 1787. [OBA.197]

MCNEIL, JAMES, emigrated from Ireland to America in 1763, settled in Bedford, Pennsylvania, a Loyalist soldier who was captured at Yorktown, Virginia, later settled at Burton, New Brunswick, in 1783. [TNA.AO12.40.262-265]

MACNEMURROW, DENNIS, a militiaman in Barbados in 1679. [TNA.CO1.44.47]

MCNICE, JAMES, a Sergeant of the Glengarry Fencibles, settled in Bastard, Ontario, on 20 October 1819. [PAO.ms154]

MACQUIN, DANIEL, emigrated from Ireland to America in 1765, settled in Ulster County, New York, a Lieutenant of Colonel Fanning's Regiment, later settled at Cataraqui by 1787. [OBA] [UEL.II.952]

MACREEDY, BRYAN, a militiaman in Barbados in 1679. [TNA.CO1.44.47]

MACSHEEHY, PATRICK, Sub Lieutenant of the Dillon Regiment, of the Irish Brigade in French Service, in America between 1778 and 1783. [IS.XIII.51]

MCSHUNY, CORNELIUS, a soldier of Captain Harrison's Company on Barbados in 1679. [TNA.CO1.44.47]

MCSHUNY, DANIEL, a soldier of Captain Harrison's Company on Barbados in 1679. [TNA.CO1.44.47]

MADDEN, MICHAEL, a soldier of the 18th [Royal Regiment of Ireland] Foot, at Charleston Heights, Massachusetts, in 1775. [TNA.WO12.3501]

MAGENNIS, H. R., a Lieutenant Colonel, at the Battle of New Orleans in 1812. [IR]

MAGRA, WILLIAM, a soldier stationed at Placentia, Newfoundland, in 1732. [TNA.CO194.24.109]

MAGROUGH, JOHN, a soldier of Captain Lewgar's Company on Barbados in 1679. [TNA.CO1.44.47]

MAHONEY, DENIS, Sub Lieutenant of the Dillon Regiment, of the Irish Brigade in French Service, in America between 1778 and 1783. [IS.XIII.51]

MAIRREN, DERMOND, a soldier of Captain Thornhill's Company on Barbados in 1679. [TNA.CO1.44.47]

MALLAHAN, DENIS, a militiaman of Captain Tim Thornhill's Company in Barbados in 1679. [TNA.CO1.44.47] [H2.80]

MALLARD, JOSEPH, from Ireland, late a Sergeant of the 70th [Surrey] Regiment, settled in Bathurst, Ontario, on 25 March 1821. [PAO.ms154]

MALLON, PATRICK, in Fintown, County Tyrone, late of the 89th [Princess Victoria's] Foot, applied to settled in Canada on 15 January 1829. [TNA.CO384.16]

MALONE, DARMOND, of Captain John Dempster's troop in Barbados in 1679 [H2.78]

MALPASS, THOMAS, a soldier of the 18th [Royal Regiment of Ireland] Foot in Philadelphia, Pennsylvania, in 1770, deserted on 23 August 1770. [TNA.WO.76/25]

MANGAN, MATTHEW, born in Ireland, a sailor in the Royal Navy, settled as a mariner in New York, a Loyalist in 1776, in London by 1786. [TNA.AO12.102.12]

MANSFIELD, Ensign THOMAS, in Montserrat in 1677-1678. [TNA]

MARTIN, JAMES, born 1722, a tailor in King George, Virginia, a soldier of Captain Henry Woodward's Company in Virginia, on 11 September 1757. [VCS]

MARRAN, DAVID, settled in St George's parish, Georgia, joined the British Army and fought at the Siege of Savannah, Georgia, later settled in Larne, Ireland, by 1785. [TNA.AO12.3.101]

MASSEY, Major, of the 27th [Inniskilling] Regiment, fought at Ticonderoga, New York, in 1759, served in Nova Scotia in 1761. [IR.35]

MATALA, Sergeant DENNIS, in Halfwaytree Division, St Kitts, on 7 February 1678. [TNA.CO1.42]

MATHESON, ALEXANDER, from Ireland, a Quarter Master Sergeant of the Glengarry Fencibles, settled in Drummond, Ontario, on 23 July 1816. [PAO.ms154]

MAW, Sergeant WILLIAM, in St Thomas, Middle Island, St Kitts, on 7 February 1678. [TNA.CO1.42]

MAWBY, GEORGE, a Volunteer of the 18th [Royal Regiment of Ireland] Foot around 1770. [PEF.186]; was appointed Ensign of the 18th Foot, on 10 December 1776. [SM.38.677]

MAWBY, GEORGE, a soldier of the 18th [Royal Regiment of Ireland] Foot, 'absent without leave' in New York in 1775. [TNA.WO.76/25]

MAWBY, JOHN, sr. Staff Officer and Adjutant of the 18th [Royal Regiment of Ireland] Foot in Philadelphia, Pennsylvania, in 1772, a Captain Lieutenant in New York in 1775; Captain Lieutenant John Mawby was promoted to be Captain of the 18th Foot on 2 February 1779. [SM.41.111][TNA.WO.76/25][PEF.210]

MAWBY, JOHN, jr. Lieutenant of the 18th [Royal Regiment of Ireland] Foot around 1770, Adjutant of the Royal Regiment of Ireland, in 1771, in New York in 1775; at Charleston Heights, Masschusetts, on 7 October 1775; a Lieutenant of the 18th Foot, was promoted to Captain on 2 February 1779. [TNA.WO.75/25; TNA.WO12.3501][PEF.170][SM.41.111]

MAWBY, SEBRIGHT, Ensign or Volunteer of the 18th [Royal Regiment of Ireland] Foot, around 1770. [PEF.188]

MAY, JOHN, a soldier of the 18th [Royal Regiment of Ireland] Foot in Philadelphia, Pennsylvania, in 1770, enlisted on 24 June 1770, and deserted on 24 September 1770. [TNA.W0.76/25]

MAY, MARTIN, born 1725 in Ireland, a blacksmith who enlisted in Captain Thomas Cocke's Company in Amelia, Virginia, on 6 January 1755. [VCS]

MEAD, MICHAEL, from Ireland, late of the 1st [Royal Scots] Regiment, settled in Lanark, Ontario, on 8 November 1820. [PAO.ms154]

MEADE, MICHAEL, from Ireland, a former Corporal of the Royal Veteran Battalion, settled in Burgess, Ontario, on 22 October 1817. [PAO.ms154]

MEEK, WILLIAM, emigrated from Ireland to America in 1768, settled in Ninety-six District, South Carolina, a Loyalist soldier during the American Revolution, moved to Rawdon, Nova Scotia. [UEL.I.184]

MEIGHAN, GEORGE, a Second Lieutenant of the Walsh Regiment, of the Irish Brigade in French Service, in America between 1778 and 1783. [IS.XIII.51]

MILES, JOHN, born 1733 in Ireland, a planter in Frederick, Virginia, a soldier in Captain Waggener's Company at Fort Holland in August 1757. [VCS]

MILLBY, alias WILLOUGHBY, ROBERT, a weaver and former dragoon of Lord Stair's Regiment, absconded from the service of Lawrence Washington on 16 August 1748. [MG.174]

MILLER, GARRET, emigrated from Ireland to America in 1772, settled in Virginia, later in Camden, Charlotte County, New York, a Loyalist soldier at Crown Point, New York, in 1776 as a Quartermaster Sergeant, moved to Sorel, Quebec, in 1783. [OBA.785]

MILLER, JAMES, settled on Jackson's Creek, Camden District, South Carolina, was appointed Captain of Militia in Charleston, S.C., moved to Ballymore, County Antrim, Ireland, by 1783. [TNA.AO12.406.202]

MILLER, JAMES, from Ireland, formerly a Sergeant of the 5th Dragoon Guards, settled in Bathurst, Ontario, on 9 August 1817. [PAO.ms154]

MILLER, JOHN, a drummer of the 18th [Royal Regiment of Ireland] Foot, in New York in 1775. [TNA.WO.76/25]

MILLER, JOHN, a schoolmaster in Camden District, South Carolina, before1780, joined the British Army at Camden, moved to Portglenone, County Antrim, Ireland, by 1783. [TNA.AO13.91.432]

MILLER WILLIAM, a soldier of the 18th [Royal Regiment of Ireland] Foot in Charlestown Heights, Massachusetts, in 1775. [TNA.WO.12.3501]

MILLOWNEY, MAURICE, late of the Glengarry Fencibles, settled in Bathurst, Ontario, on 23 July 1816. [PAO.ms154]

MIHAN, ANDREW, in Temps, County, Fermanagh, an army pensioner, applied to settle in Canada on 24 March 1827. [TNA.CO384.16]

MINNER, WILLIAM, a soldier of the 18th [Royal Regiment of Ireland] Foot in Philadelphia, Pennsylvania, in 1772. [TNA.W0.76/25]

MITCHELL, DANIEL, formerly a soldier of the 88th [Connaught] Regiment, settled in Drummond, Ontario, on 14 July 1816. [PAO.ms154]

MITCHELL, Lieutenant Colonel EDWARD, of the 52nd [Oxfordshire] Regiment, was appointed Lieutenant Colonel of the 27th Regiment on 20 January 1777. [SM.40.55]

MITCHELL, JOHN, a soldier of the 18th [Royal Regiment of Ireland] Foot in Philadelphia, Pennsylvania, in 1767. [TNA.WO.76/25]

MITCHEL, JOHN, born 1836, son of John Mitchel [1815-1875], emigrated to America in 1853, was killed in action while commanding Fort Sumner, South Carolina, for the Confederates in 1864. [NLI.mss3225-3226]

MITCHELL, ROBERT, a soldier of the 18th [Royal Regiment of Ireland] Foot in Philadelphia, Pennsylvania, in 1767. [TNA.WO.76/25]

MOLOHANE, JOHN, a militiaman in Barbados in 1679. [TNA.CO1.44.47]

MOLONEY, EDMUND, an officer of the Royal Irish Artillery who died in the West Indies, possibly as a prisoner of war in 1794. [IS.XVI]

MONCREIFF, THOMAS, from Dungannon, a Major in British service in New York, probate, July 1792, PCC. [TNA]

MONEYPENNY, WILLIAM, a soldier of the 18th [Royal Regiment of Ireland] Foot, at Charleston Heights, Massachusetts, in 1775. [TNA.WO12.3501]

MONTGOMERY, JOHN, of Ballevegley, County Antrim, fought at the Battle of Dunbar on 1 September 1650, and at the Siege of Worcester in September 1651 where he was captured and transported to Virginia, a petition in 1661. [SP.Ire.306/959; SP.Ire.1661.242]

MONTGOMERY, RICHARD, born 1736 in Donegal, an Ensign of the 17th [The Loyal Irish] Regiment of Foot, fought at the Siege of Quebec in 1759, also in Martinique and Havanna, Cuba, settled at Rhinebeck, New York, in 1772, a Brigadier General of the American Army who was killed in an attack on Quebec in 1775. [PRONI.T1023][DCB]

MORGAN, JOHN BAPTISTE, Sub Lieutenant of the Dillon Regiment, of the Irish Brigade in French Service, in America between 1778 and 1783. [IS.XIII.51]

MOOR, EDWARD, a soldier of the 18th [Royal Regiment of Ireland] Foot, in Charlestown Heights, Massachusetts, died on 6 July 1775. [TNA.WO.12.3801]

MOORE, GERARD, Captain of the Dillon Regiment, of the Irish Brigade in French Service, in America between 1778 and 1783. [IS.XIII.51]

MOORE, Lieutenant HENRY, of the 27th [Inniskilling] Regiment, was promoted to Captain of the said regiment, on 7 April 1777. [SM.40.223]

MOORE, JAMES, emigrated from Belfast, Ireland, aboard the Pennsylvania Farmer bound to Charleston, South Carolina, in 1772, a storekeeper there, served in Colonel Thomas Brown's Rangers until they were disbanded in 1783, then moved to Nova Scotia. [TNA.AO12.52.169]

MOORE, JOHN, born 1728 in Ireland, enlisted in Captain Christopher Gist's Company in Frederick, Virginia, on 2 February 1756. [VCS]

MOORE, General JOHN, of the 27th [Inniskilling] Foot, captured St Lucia in May 1756, also Fort Charlotte, St Lucia, in 1796. [IR.47]

MOORE, ROBERT, formerly a Sergeant of the 104th Regiment, settled in Bathurst, Ontario, on 17 December 1819. [PAO.ms154]

MOORE, SAMUEL, a soldier of the 27th [Inniskilling] Regiment, at Fort George, New York, on 4 September 1757. [NRS.GD45.2.35.2]

MOORE, WILLIAM, born in Ireland, served as a soldier in the French and Indians War from 1757, was appointed Colonel of the Camden District Militia during the War of Independence, moved to London by 1786 but wished to return to Ireland. [TNA.AO12.3.205]

MOORE, WILLIAM, Captain of the Dillon Regiment, of the Irish Brigade in French Service, in America between 1778 and 1783. [IS.XIII.51]

MOORE, WILLIAM, an officer of the Royal Irish Artillery, died in the West Indies on 23 July 1796. [IS.XVI]

MOORE, WILLIAM, from Ireland, formerly a driver of the Royal Artillery, settled in Drummond, Ontario, on 26 October 1816. [PAO.ms154]

MOORIN, DOMINICK, born 1733 in Ireland, a joiner in Essex, Virginia, a soldier of Captain Henry Woodward's Company in Virginia, on 11 September 1757. [VCS]

MORRIS, Major APOLLO, attempted to act as peacemaker between George Washington and William Howe in 1777. [TCD. Conolly pp]

MORRIS, WILLIAM, a soldier of the 18th [Royal Regiment of Ireland] Foot in Philadelphia, Pennsylvania, in 1767. [TNA.WO.76/25]

MOTT, CHARLES, a soldier of the 18th [Royal Regiment of Ireland] Foot in Philadelphia, Pennsylvania, in 1770; in New York in 1775. [TNA.WO.76/25]

MULBOY, WILLIAM, a soldier of the 18th [Royal Regiment of Ireland] Foot, in Philadelphia, Pennsylvania, in 1771, transferred to Lieutenant Colonel's Company on 8 April 1771. [TNA.WO.76/25]

MULLARONEY, MAURICE, from Ireland, formerly a private of the Glengarry Fencibles, settled in Drummond, Ontario, on 23 July 1816. [PAO.ms154]

MULLEN, PETER, born 1733 in Ireland, a labourer, who enlisted in Captain David Bell's Company of Militia, in Virginia, on 12 May 1756. [VCS]

MULLINS, PATRICK, from Ireland, late of the 27th [Inniskilling] Regiment, settled in Drummond, Ontario, on 17 December 1817. [PAO.ms154]

MULLINS, THOMAS, a soldier of Captain Hall's Company on Barbados in 1679. [TNA.CO1.44.47]

MURDESHOW, JOHN, a soldier of the 18th [Royal Regiment of Ireland] Foot in Philadelphia, Pennsylvania, in 1767. [TNA.WO.76/25]

MURPHY, CORNELIUS, born 1792, enlisted in the British Army in Kilbrogan, County Cork, in 1813, was discharged in Fredericton, New Brunswick, in 1818, settled in Dalhousie, Nova Scotia, in 1820. [TNA.WO.25.548]

MURPHY, DANIEL, a militiaman in Captain Timothy Thornhill's Company on Barbados in 1679. [TNA.CO.44.47] [H2.80]

MURPHY, DENNIS, born in County Wexford, emigrated to Halifax, Nova Scotia, in 1791, a militiaman there until 1795, moved to Port Hood, Cape Breton, Nova Scotia in 1819. [NSARM.mf15792/6]

MURPHY, EDWARD, from Ireland, formerly Quartermaster of the Royal Newfoundland Regiment, settled in Drummond, Ontario, on 19 January 1819. [PAO.ms154]

MURPHY, FRANCIS, born in County Monaghan, emigrated to Cape Breton, Nova Scotia, in 1785, a magistrate and Captain of Militia, settled at Grand Grave, St Peter's Bay, N.S., in 1812. [NSARM.mf16701]

MURPHY, Captain JAMES, a merchant in Talbot County, Maryland, by 1689. [MSA.24.171]

MURPHY, JAMES, settled in Ninety-Six District, South Carolina, about 1781, joined the British Army in 1779, moved to London by 1783. [TNA.AO12.46.233]

MURPHY, JOHN, emigrated from Ireland to America in 1773, settled in Ninety-six District, South Carolina, a Loyalist soldier who moved to Rawdon, Nova Scotia. [UEL.I.695]

MURPHY, LAURENCE, a soldier of the 18th [Royal Regiment of Ireland] Foot in New York in 1775. [TNA.W0.76/25]

MURPHY, MARTIN, from Ireland, formerly a private of the 37th [North Hampshire] Regiment, settled in Drummond, Ontario, on 16 July 1816. [PAO.ms154]

MURPHY, MICHAEL, from Ireland, formerly a private of the Glengarry Fencibles, settled in Drummond, Ontario, on 16 July 1816. [PAO.ms154]

MURPHY, MORRIS, a militiaman in Captain John Sampson's Company on Barbados in 1679. [H2.79]

MURPHY, MORGAN, a soldier of Colonel Thornhill's Company on Barbados in 1679. [TNA.CO1.44.47]

MURPHY, PATRICK, Sub Lieutenant of the Dillon Regiment, of the Irish Brigade in French Service, in America between 1778 and 1783. [IS.XIII.51]

MURPHY, ROBERT, a soldier of the 18th [Royal Regiment of Ireland] Foot in Philadelphia, Pennsylvania, in 1770, in New York in 1775. [TNA.W0.76/25]

MURPHY, ROBERT, emigrated from Ireland to America, for 38 years was a planter and merchant in America, based at Broad River, South Carolina, a Loyalist soldier who fought in the Carolinas notably at Eutaw, died in England, probate 27 November 1786 PCC. [TNA]

MURPHY, THOMAS, a soldier of Colonel Harrison's Company on Barbados in 1679. [TNA.CO1.44.47]

MURPHY, THOMAS, late of the Royal Sappers, settled in Lanark, Ontario, on 1 November 1820. [PAO.ms154]

MURPHY, WILLIAM, a former Sergeant of the Canadian Fencibles, settled in Kitley, Ontario, on 25 October 1819. [PAO.ms154]

MURPHY, ..., formerly a private of the Prince of York's Chasseurs, settled in Drummond, Ontario, on 1 October 1819. [PAO.ms154]

MURPHY, ..., formerly Quartermaster of the Prince of York's Chasseurs, settled in Drummond, Ontario, on 1 October 1819. [PAO.ms154]

MURRAY, Sir JAMES, served in the Army between 1756 and 1763, a Lieutenant by 1772, fought in America and notably in the defence of St Kitts, died 26 April 1811.

MURRAY, Major WILLIAM, of the 42nd [Royal Highland – Black Watch] Regiment, was appointed the Lieutenant Colonel of the 27th [Inniskilling] Regiment on 20 January 1777. [SM.40.55], of the 27th Foot, was promoted to Lieutenant Colonel of that regiment on 20 January 1778. [SM.40.54]

MURRAY, WILLIAM, from Ireland, formerly a private of the 88th Connaught] Regiment, settled in Beckwith, Ontario, on 28 February 1817. [PAO.ms154]

MURRAY, WILLIAM, formerly a Sergeant of the Canadian Fencibles, settled in Beckwith, Ontario, on 25 November 1819. [PAO.ms154]

MUSGRAVE, WILLIAM, a soldier of the 18th [Royal Regiment of Ireland] Foot in Philadelphia, Pennsylvania, in 1767; a Sergeant of the 18th Foot in Charlestown Heights, Massachusetts, in 1775. [TNA.WO.12.3501; WO.76/25]

NAGLE, JAMES, a Captain of the Walsh Regiment, of the Irish Brigade in French Service, in America between 1778 and 1783. [IS.XIII.51]

NAMOCK, WILLIAM, a soldier of the 18th [Royal Regiment of Ireland] Foot in Charlestown Heights, Massachusetts, deserted on 25 January 1775. [TNA.WO.12.3801]

NASH, MARTIN, from Goran, County Kilkenny, a former soldier of the 37th [North Hampshire] Regiment, settled at Rideau, Canada, in 1820. [PAC.RG8.b22894/49]

NEALE, Captain JAMES, in Charles County, Maryland, by 1683. [MSA.25.1]

NEALL, DANIEL, a soldier of the 18th [Royal Regiment of Ireland] Foot in Philadelphia, Pennsylvania, in 1767, a Corporal, later Sergeant, at Charleston Heights, Massachusetts., in 1775. [TNA.WO.76/25]

NEALL, JAMES, born 1733 in Ireland, a clerk in Stafford, Virginia, a soldier of Captain Henry Woodward's Company in Virginia, on 11 September 1757. [VCS]

NEILSON, ARTHUR SCOTT, emigrated from Ireland to America aged 11 years, a merchant in New Brunswick, New Jersey, he joined the Royal Navy around 1776 and served until discharged in 1781, in London in 1783. [TNA.AO.12.99.24]

NELE, DERBY, a Militiaman of Captain Woodward's Company in Barbados in 1679. [TNA.CO1.44.47] [H2.156]

NELSON, EDWARD, a soldier of the 18th [Royal Regiment of Ireland] Foot in Philadelphia, Pennsylvania, in 1767. [TNA.WO.76/25; WO.12.3501]

NEWBURGH, ROBERT JOCELYN, Staff Officer of the 18th [Royal Regiment of Ireland] Foot from 1740 until 1802, a chaplain in New York in 1775. [TNA.WO.76/25][PEF.213]

NICKELS, JAMES, emigrated from Ireland to America in 1773, settled at Mud Lick Creek, Ninety-six District, South Carolina, a Loyalist in Colonel Turner's Corps, later Captain of Militia. [UEL.I.169]

NODD, JAMES, a soldier of the 18th [Royal Regiment of Ireland] Foot in Philadelphia, Pennsylvania, in 1767. [TNA.WO.76/25]

NOLAN, PATRICK, from Ireland, late a Lieutenant of the Canadian Fencibles, settled in Drummond, Ontario, on 16 November 1816. [PAO.ms154]

NORRIS, RICHARD, a Lieutenant of the 17th [The Loyal Irish] Regiment, to be Captain of the 27th [Inniskilling] Regiment on 3 November 1778. [SM.40.631]

NOVOLAN, CHRISTOPHER, Second Captain of the Dillon Regiment, of the Irish Brigade in French Service, in America between 1778 and 1783. [IS.XIII.51]

NUGENT, ANSELME, Captain of the Dillon Regiment, of the Irish Brigade in French Service, in America between 1778 and 1783. [IS.XIII.51]

NUGENT, EDMOND, an officer of the Royal Irish Artillery, died in the West Indies on 11 May 1794. [IS.XVI]

NUGENT, EDWARD, a soldier under Captain Ralph Lane at Roanoke, Carolina, in 1586.

NUGENT, General Sir GEORGE, Governor and Commander in Chief of Jamaica, papers, 1802-1805. [RUSI.MM183A-183D]

NUGENT, Captain WALTER, of the Royal Marines, died in New York in 1776. [SM.38.622]

NUTTERFIELD, ..., a Lieutenant of the 27th [Inniskilling] Regiment, in the Fort George, New York, on 4 September 1757. [NRS.GD45.2.35.2]

O'BERIN, MICHAEL, Captain of the Dillon Regiment, of the Irish Brigade in French Service, in America between 1778 and 1783. [IS.XIII.51]

O'BRIAN, ARTHUR, born 5 August 1810 at Cove of Cork, an Ensign who died in Dominica on 24 May 1838. [IG.8.2.271]

O'BRYAN, DANIEL, a soldier stationed at Placentia, Newfoundland, in 1732. [TNA.CO194.24.10 9]

O'BRYAN, DANIEL, a soldier of Captain Maunsell's Company at Albany, New York, on 24 September 1757. [NRS.GD45.2.35.4]

O'BRYAN, DANIEL, a soldier of the 2nd Battalion of the 84th [Royal Highland Emigrants] Regiment, aboard the frigate Raleigh bound from New York to Charleston, South Carolina, in 1780. [NRS.GD174.2405]

O'BRIEN, Colonel JAMES, in Port Royal, Jamaica, probate, 27 April 1692, Cork Diocesan Court. [Inchiquin Manuscript number 1496]

O'BRIEN, J. H., formerly an Ensign of the Royal Newfoundland Fencibles, settled in Drummond, Ontario, on 26 June 1817. [PAO.ms154]

O'BRYEN, JOHN, born 1778, enlisted in the British Army in County Mayo in 1813, discharged in St John in 1818, settled in Dalhousie, Nova Scotia, in 1820. [TNA.WO25.548]

O'BRIEN, JOSEPH, from Ireland, formerly an Ensign, settled in Elmsley and Beckwith, Ontario, on 30 November 1816. [PAO.ms154]

O'BRIAN, MORRIS, a Militiaman of Captain Samuel Woodward's Company on Barbados in 1679. [TNA.CO1.44.47] [H2.156]

O'BRIAN, THADEUS, Major of the Walsh Regiment, of the Irish Brigade in French Service, in America between 1778 and 1783. [IS.XIII.51]

O'BRUDY, TEAGUE, a soldier under the command of Captain Robert Bowcher on Barbados on 6 January 1679. [HS.82]

O'CAHILL, LOUIS, a Second Lieutenant of the Walsh Regiment, of the Irish Brigade in French Service, in America between 1778 and 1783. [IS.XIII.51]

O'CALLAGHAN, Mrs, wife of Staff Sergeant O'Callaghan, now of the 27th [Innerkilling] Regiment, died on Trinidad in 1828. [Kilkenny Independent.10.5.1828]

O'CONNELL, MORRIS, a soldier or militiaman in Colonel Lyne's Regiment on Barbados in 1679. [H2.112]

O'CONNOR, Captain ARMAND, of Walsh's Regiment in the French Army, participated in the capture of Tobago and St Eustatius in 1781. [IS.XIII/XIV]

O'CONNOR, ..., possibly late of the Prince of York's Chasseurs, settled in Drummond, Ontario, on 1 October 1819. [PAO.ms154]

O'CROLY, CHARLES, a Captain of the Walsh Regiment, of the Irish Brigade in French Service, in America between 1778 and 1783. [IS.XIII.51]

O'CROWLEY, FELIX, a Second Lieutenant of the Walsh Regiment, of the Irish Brigade in French Service, in America between 1778 and 1783. [IS.XIII.51]

O'DOYER, DENIS, Second Captain of the Dillon Regiment, of the Irish Brigade in French Service, in America between 1778 and 1783. [IS.XIII.51]

O'DRISCOLL, JAMES, a Captain of the Walsh Regiment, of the Irish Brigade in French Service, in America between 1778 and 1783. [IS.XIII.51]

O'FARREL, CLAUDE, Lieutenant of the Dillon Regiment, of the Irish Brigade in French Service, in America between 1778 and 1783. [IS.XIII.51]

O'FARRELL, EMANUEL, Second Lieutenant of the Dillon Regiment, of the Irish Brigade in French Service, in America between 1778 and 1783. [IS.XIII.51]

O'FARRELL, JAMES, Second Lieutenant of the Dillon Regiment, of the Irish Brigade in French Service, in America between 1778 and 1783. [IS.XIII.51]

O'FLYN, JAMES, a Second Lieutenant of the Walsh Regiment, of the Irish Brigade in French Service, in America between 1778 and 1783. [IS.XIII.51]

O'GORMAN, CHARLES, a Second Lieutenant of the Walsh Regiment, of the Irish Brigade in French Service, in America between 1778 and 1783. [IS.XIII.51]

O'HARA, CHARLES, Colonel of the Coldstream Guards, was appointed Brigadier in North America from 30 April 1780. [HMC. American. ii.121]; was wounded at Camden, South Carolina, in March 1781. [HMC. American.ii.261]

O'HARA, THOMAS, late Sergeant of the Glengarry Fencibles, settled in Burgess, Ontario, on 26 September 1816. [PAO.ms154]

O'HEARA, THOMAS, from Ireland, a former Sergeant of the Glengarry Fencibles, settled in Leeds, Ontario, on 31 July 1817. [PAO.ms154]

O'HIGGINS, TOMAS, a Captain of Dragoons in Chile in 1795, Governor of Juan Fernandez in 1804, and Colonel of the Independence Army in 1812. [ISE.289]

O'HOWLEY, FFLAN, sr., a soldier of Captain Liston's Company on Barbados in 1679. [TNA.CO1.44.47]

O'HOWLEY, FFLAN, jr., a soldier of Captain Liston's Company on Barbados in 1679. [TNA.CO1.44.47]

O'KEEFFE, DANIEL, Captain of the Royal York Rangers, died in Barbados on 24 June 1818. [St Michael's Cathedral gravestone, Bridgetown, Barbados]

O'KEEFE, PATRICK, Lieutenant of the Dillon Regiment, of the Irish Brigade in French Service, in America between 1778 and 1783. [IS.XIII.51]

O'HARA, General CHARLES, son of James O'Hara of Tyrawley, Ireland, at Yorktown, Virginia, in 1776; a letter dated 4 July 1782 from St John's, Antigua. [HMC.American.iii.6]

O'MALLEY, THOMAS, a British Army physician from 1801 to 1806, graduated MD from St Andrews University in 1816, Health Officer of St Kitts. [St AUR]

O'MEARA, DANIEL, Sub Lieutenant of the Dillon Regiment, of the Irish Brigade in French Service, in America between 1778 and 1783. [IS.XIII.51]

O'MEARA, JOHN BAPTISTE, a Second Lieutenant of the Walsh Regiment, of the Irish Brigade in French Service, in America between 1778 and 1783. [IS.XIII.51]

O'MORAN, CHARLES, Sub Lieutenant of the Dillon Regiment, of the Irish Brigade in French Service, in America between 1778 and 1783. [IS.XIII.51]

O'MORAN, JAMES, Major of the Dillon Regiment, of the Irish Brigade in French Service, in America between 1778 and 1783. [IS.XIII.51]

O'NEALE, Don CARLOS FELIX, born 1681, son of Sir Neil O'Neale of Ulster who died at the Battle of the Boyne in 1690, a Lieutenant General in Spanish Service and former Governor of Havanna, Cuba, died in Madrid, Spain, on 10 September 1791. [SM.53.517]

O'NEILL. BERNARD, Captain of the Dillon Regiment, of the Irish Brigade in French Service, in America between 1778 and 1783. [IS.XIII.51]

O'NEILL, JAMES, in Granard, County Longford, late of the West India Rangers, applied to settle in Canada on 20 March 1827. [TNA.CO384.16]

O'NEIL, JOHN, a Captain of the Walsh Regiment, of the Irish Brigade in French Service, in America between 1778 and 1783. [IS.XIII.51]

O'NEIL, MICHAEL, born 1727 in Ireland, a planter in Frederick, Virginia, a soldier in Captain Robert Spotswood's Company at Fort Young in 1757. [VCS]

O'NEILL, PATRICK, born 1797, enlisted in the British Army in County Tipperary in 1813, was discharged in Fredericton, New Brunswick, in 1818, settled in Dalhousie, Nova Scotia, in 1820. [TNA.WO.25.548]

O'NEILL, WILLIAM, born 1774, enlisted in the British Army in Kilkenny in 1805, was discharged in St John, Newfoundland, in 1818, settled in Dalhousie, Nova Scotia, in 1820. [TNA.WO.25.548]

O'NELE, DARBY, a militiaman in Captain John Sampson's Company on Barbados in 1679. [H2.79]

ORAN, ..., a former Sergeant of the Prince of York's Chasseurs, settled in Drummond, Ontario, on 1 October 1819. [PAO.ms154]

O'REILLY, ALEXANDER, born 1723 in County Meath, joined the Spanish Army, a Brigadier General of the Spanish Army in Cuba and Puerto Rico, was appointed Governor and Captain General of 'Spanish Louisiana, in 1769, died 1794 in Cadiz, Spain; reference to his wanton cruelties on the French inhabitants of Louisiana, in a letter from St Augustine, East Florida, dated 23 February 1783. [HMC. American.iii.367]; 'O'RILEY, General', attacked Pensacola in December 1779. [HMC. American ii .77]

O'REILLY, CHARLES, Sub Lieutenant of the Dillon Regiment, of the Irish Brigade in French Service, in America between 1778 and 1783. [IS.XIII.51]

O'REILLY, JOHN, Second Captain of the Dillon Regiment, of the Irish Brigade in French Service, in America between 1778 and 1783. [IS.XIII.51]

O'RIORDAN, JAMES, a Lieutenant of the Walsh Regiment, of the Irish Brigade in French Service, in America between 1778 and 1783. [IS.XIII.51]

O'SHIEL, JAMES, a Second Lieutenant of the Walsh Regiment, of the Irish Brigade in French Service, in America between 1778 and 1783. [IS.XIII.51]

OSBORN, WILLIAM, a soldier of the 18th [Royal Regiment of Ireland] Foot in New York in 1775. [TNA.WO.76/25]

O'SULLIVAN, Captain FLORENCE, raised a company of soldiers in Barbados to regain St Kitts but was captured and imprisoned by the French 'in the island of Tothus Santus', a petition dated 1668. [PCCol.1668.741; PCCol.1668.741/788]

OWENS, HENRY, Sub Lieutenant of the Dillon Regiment, of the Irish Brigade in French Service, in America between 1778 and 1783. [IS.XIII.51]

OWENS, JOHN, a soldier of the 18th [Royal Regiment of Ireland] Foot in Philadelphia, Pennsylvania, in 1770, deserted on 23 August 1770. [TNA.WO.76/25]

OWENS, WILLIAM, emigrated from Ireland to America in 1774, settled as a gunsmith in Frederick Town, Maryland, a Corporal of the Maryland Loyalists Regiment, he returned to Ireland. [TNA.AO12.100.310]

PAKENHAM, Sir EDWARD, born 1777, second son of Lord Longford, as Colonel of the 64th Regiment he spent years fighting in the West Indies, then fought at New Orleans where he was killed in 1815. [IS.IX.36]

PALMER, WILLIAM, from Ireland, late a private of the 104th [North British] Regiment, settled in Burgess, Ontario, on 30 June 1817. [PAO.ms154]

PARKER, LAURENCE, late of the Glengarry Fencibles, settled in Drummond, Ontario, on 16 July 1816. [PAO.ms154]

PARKER, WILLIAM, a soldier of the 18th [Royal Regiment of Ireland] Foot in Philadelphia, Pennsylvania, in 1771. [TNA.WO.76/25]

PATERSON, DAVID, from Ireland, a former soldier, settled in Beckwith, Ontario, on 7 March 1817. [PAO.ms154]

PATERSON, MARCUS, a Lieutenant of the 18th [Royal Regiment of Ireland] Foot around 1770. [PEF.172]

PATTERSON, RICHARD, from Ireland, a former private of the 23rd [Royal Welch Fusiliers] Regiment, settled in Bathurst, Ontario, on 31 July 1817. [PAO.ms154]

PATTERSON, WALTER, born in Rathmelton, County Donegal, around 1735, an Ensign of the 80th [Staffordshire] Regiment of Foot in 1757, served under Abercromby at Ticonderoga in 1758, and under Amherst on Lake Champlain, later a land speculator on Prince Edward Island where he became Governor in 1769, he died in London on 6 September 1798. [DCB]

PATRICK, MATTHEW, a former Sergeant of the 3rd Dragoons, settled in Beckwith, Ontario, on 18 September 1819. [PAO.ms154]

PAYNE, BENJAMIN CHARNOCK, Captain or Captain Lieutenant of the 18th [Royal Regiment of Ireland] Foot, in New York in 1775. [PEF.128]

PEAVIS, RICHARD, emigrated from Ireland to America aged 10 years, settled on the Enoe River, South Carolina, in 1775, later on the St John's River in Florida in 1783, served as a Loyalist Colonel during the American Revolution. [UEL.I.191]

PENEFATHER, JOHN, possibly from Ireland, settled in Charleston, South Carolina, commander of Fort Johnson, probate 21 February 1745, South Carolina.

PERKINS, WILLIAM, Lieutenant of the 18th [Royal Regiment of Ireland] Foot in Philadelphia, Pennsylvania, in 1767. [TNA.WO.76/25][PEF.173]

PHIBBS, ORMSBY, born 1806, Lieutenant Colonel of the 88th [Connaught] Regiment, died of yellow fever in Barbados on 17 January 1848. [St Paul's monumental inscription]

PHILLIPS, RALPH, late of Savannah River, South Carolina, a former Major of the 85th [Royal Volunteers] Regiment of Foot who had served from 1755 until 1781, settled in County Donegal, Ireland, by 1788. [TNA.AO12.92.1a]

PHILLIPS, ..., from Ireland, formerly in the Royal Navy, settled in Drummond, Ontario, on 21 December 1818. [PAO.ms154]

PHIPOE, THOMAS, emigrated from Ireland to Charleston, South Carolina, in 1771, a lawyer, Colonel of Loyalist Militia in Charleston in 1780. [UEL.II.1174]

PIERCY, JOHN, an Ensign of the 18th [Royal Regiment of Scotland] Foot around 1770. [PEF.191]

PITT, SIMON, a soldier of the 18th [Royal Regiment of Ireland] Foot, in New York in 1775. [TNA.WO.76/25]

PLACKETT, JOHN, born 1731 in Ireland, a planter in Frederick, Virginia, a soldier in Colonel George Washington's Company in 1757. [VCS]

PLUNKETT, FRANCIS, a Lieutenant of the Walsh Regiment, of the Irish Brigade in French Service, in America between 1778 and 1783. [IS.XIII.51]

PLUNKETT, JOHN, a militiaman of Captain Thomas Helm Company in Barbados in 1679. [TNA.CO1.44.47] [H2.153]

PLUNKETT, THOMAS, born 1785 in Wexford, enlisted in the 95th Rifles in 1805, took part in the River Plate Campaign and fought at the Battle of Buenos Ayres, Argentina, 1806-1807, later fought at the Battle of Waterloo in 1815, enrolled in the 41st [Welch] Regiment, briefly settled in Canada, died in Colchester, England, in 1839.

PLUNKETT, Captain in Guadaloupe in 1652. [HMC.36; Ormonde ns 1.163]

POMEROY, General JOHN, a diary of his voyage with the 64th [Staffordshire] Foot to North America in September 1768; also, a letter from J. Stuart dated 6 July 1775 with an account of the Battle of Bunker Hill. [PRONI.T2954]

POWELL, JAMES H., from Ireland, late Major of the 103rd Regiment, settled in Drummond, Ontario, on 22 June 1822. [PAO.ms154]

POWER, Sir MANLY, from Montreal, Quebec, with the 1st Battalion of the 27th [Inniskilling] Regiment bound for New Orleans to reinforce the army there in November 1815. [IR.67]

POWER, MAURICE, from Ireland, formerly a soldier, settled in Drummond, Ontario, on 14 October 1816. [PAO.ms154]

POWER, RICHARD, a soldier stationed at Placentia, Newfoundland, in 1732. [TNA.CO194.24.109]

POWERS, RICHARD, born 1736 in Ireland, a tailor in Suffolk County, Virginia, a soldier in Captain Robert Spotswood's Company at Fort Young in 1757. [VCS]

POYNTON, BRERETON, a Cornet of the 6th [Inniskilling] Dragoon Regiment by 1755, then an Ensign and Lieutenant of the 62nd [Wiltshire] Regiment, later in the 60th [Royal American] Regiment, fought at the Siege of Louisbourg and elsewhere in Canada to the West Indies with the 60th [Royal American] Regiment, finally a Captain of the 21st [Royal North British Fusiliers] Regiment, in London by 1784. [TNA.AO12.13.302]

PRENDERGAST, CHARLES, formerly a private of the Glengarry Fencibles, settled in Drummond, Ontario, on 17 July 1816. [PAO.ms154]

PRENDERGAST, JAMES, born 1789, from County Monaghan, an Army Lieutenant who settled in Canada, he died in 1834. [PRONI.T2410; D729]

PRENDERGAST, THOMAS, a Lieutenant stationed at Placentia, Newfoundland, in 1732. [TNA.CO194.24.109]

PRIDEAUX, EDMUND, a Lieutenant of the 18th [Royal Regiment of Ireland] Foot around 1770. [PEF.173]

PRINGLE, H., at Fort Carillon, Lake George, New York, fought in the French and Indian War, a letter to Colonel Haviland in Fort Edward dated March 1758. [PRONI.T2095]

PRINGLE, WILLIAM, formerly a private of the Glengarry Fencibles, settled in Drummond, Ontario, on 18 July 1816. [PAO.ms154]

PROCTOR, WILLIAM, a soldier of the 18th [Royal Regiment of Ireland] Foot in Philadelphia, Pennsylvania, in 1767. [TNA.WO.76/25]

PURCELL, EDWARD, born 1731 in Ireland, a planter in Hampshire, Virginia, a soldier of Captain Thomas Waggener's Company at Fort Holland in 1757. [VCS]

PURDON, HENRY, Sub Lieutenant of the Dillon Regiment, of the Irish Brigade in French Service, in America between 1778 and 1783. [IS.XIII.51]

PURDON, SIMON, Captain of the Dillon Regiment, of the Irish Brigade in French Service, in America between 1778 and 1783. [IS.XIII.51]

PURVES, Sir ALEXANDER, was appointed Major of the 18th [Royal Regiment of Ireland] Foot on 30 October 1779, [SM.41.575]; later as Colonel of the 18th Regiment on 17 November 1780. [NRS.GD158.408]

PYERAH, JOSEPH, a Sergeant of the 18th [Royal Regiment of Ireland] Foot in Philadelphia, Pennsylvania, in 1770, in New York in 1775. [TNA.WO.76/25]

QUAIL, JAMES, from Ireland, a former Sergeant of the Royal Artillery, settled in Drummond, Ontario, on 22 August 1817, later in Leeds, Ontario, on 30 November 1817. [PAO.ms154]

QUHAN, PAUL, born 1732 in Ireland, a seaman who enlisted in Captain Thomas Cocke's Company in Stafford, Virginia, on 12 September 1755. [VCS]

QUIGLEY, JAMES, late Sergeant of the Glengarry Fencibles, settled in Drummond, Ontario, on 16 July 1816. [PAO.ms154]

QUIN, JOHN, emigrated from Ireland to America in 1766, settled in Johnstown, Tryon County, New York, in 1772, a Loyalist soldier in Sir John Johnson's Regiment, [the King's Royal Regiment of New York], from 1776 until 1783, then settled in Quebec. [UEL.I.375]

QUIN, MICHAEL, emigrated from Ireland to America in 1766, settled in Johnstown, Tryon County, New York, in 1772, a Loyalist soldier in Sir John Johnson's Regiment, [the King's Royal Regiment of New York], from 1776 until 1783, then settled in Cornwall, Canada. [UEL.I.375]

QULTY, JOHN, born 1775, enlisted in the British Army in Limerick in 1804, discharged in St John in 1818, settled in Dalhousie, Nova Scotia, in 1820. [TNA.WO25.548]

READ, WILLIAM, emigrated from Ireland to America, settled at Bison Creek, parish of St George, Georgia, in 1769, a Loyalist soldier of the Florida Rangers, later Captain of the Georgia Militia, settled on the Gut of Canso, Canada. [UEL.I.581]

REGAN, JOHN, from Ireland, formerly a private of the Glengarry Fencibles, settled in Drummond, Ontario, on 16 July 1816. [PAO.ms154]

REILLY, EDWARD, from Ireland, formerly a Sergeant of the Glengarry Regiment, settled in Bathurst, Ontario, on 7 June 1818. [PAO.ms154]

RICE, JOHN, from Ireland, formerly an army Sergeant, settled in Drummond, Ontario, on 15 October 1816. [PAO.ms154]

RICE, JOHN, from Ireland, formerly a Sergeant of the Royal Newfoundland Fencibles, settled in Young, Ontario, on 31 July 1817. [PAO.ms154]

RICE, PATRICK, late of the Glengarry Fencibles, settled in Drummond, Ontario, on 16 July 1816. [PAO.ms154]

RICHARDSON, WILLIAM, a Captain of the 18th [Royal Regiment of Ireland] Foot, around 1770. [PEF.135]

RICHIE, WELLESLEY, from Ireland, a former Sergeant of the 90th [Perthshire] Regiment, settled in Elmsley, Ontario, on 31 July 1817. [PAO.ms154]

RILEY, JOHN, born 1731 in Ireland, a farmer in Augusta, Virginia, a soldier in Major Andrew Lewis's Company in Virginia in 1757. [VCS]

RIVINGTON, THOMAS, from Ireland, formerly a private of the Glengarry Fencibles, settled in Drummond, Ontario, on 16 July 1816. [PAO.ms154]

ROBINSON, JAMES, formerly of the Prince of York's Chasseurs, settled in Bathurst, Ontario, on 21 October 1819. [PAO.ms154]

ROBINSON, THOMAS, late of the 8th [King's] Regiment, settled in Bathurst, Ontario, on 6 August 1819. [PAO.ms154]

ROBINSON, WILLIAM, late of the 3rd Battalion of the Sappers and Miners, settled in Drummond, Ontario, on 30 September 1817. [PAO.ms154]

ROCHE, Sir BOYLE, an officer at the Siege of Havanna, Cuba, in 1762-died in Dublin in 1807. [SM.69/479]

ROSS, ROBERT, born 1766 in County Down, as a Major General sent to America in 1814, fought at the battles of Bladenburg, of Baltimore, and at North Point where he was killed on 12 September 1814.

ROURKE, PATRICK, from Ireland, late private of the 81st [Loyal Lincolnshire Volunteers] Regiment, settled in Beckworth, Ontario, on 14 March 1818. [PAO.ms154]

ROURKE, PATRICK, for 9 years a soldier of the 81st [Loyal Lincolnshire Volunteers] Foot, applied to settle in Canada on 15 August 1827. [TNA.CO384.16]

ROURKE, PATRICK, for 17 years a soldier of the 17TH Lancers applied to settle in Canada on 15 March 1827. [TNA.CO384.16]

ROURKE, THOMAS, for 14 years a soldier of the 4TH Light Dragoons, applied to settle in Canada on 15 August 1827. [TNA.CO384.16]

RUSSELL, JOHN, of the Grenadier Company of the 18th [Royal Regiment of Ireland] Foot, arrived in America on 11 July 1767, served at Fort Pitt, Fort Chartres, Cahokie, Philadelphia, New York, and Boston, and was killed in action near Lexington, Massachusetts, on 19 April 1775. [TNA]

RUTHERFORD, Lieutenant ARCHIBALD, of the 22nd [Cheshire] Regiment was appointed Captain of the 27th [Inniskilling] Foot, in place of William Parker, on 15 March 1777. [SM.39.168] [TNA.WO17.124]

RYAN, PHILLIP, from Ireland, late Adjutant of the 10th [North Lincoln] Regiment, settled in Montague, Oxford, Ontario, on 16 March 1818. [PAO.ms154]

RYAN, ..., formerly a private of the 37th [North Hampshire] Regiment, settled in Bathurst, Ontario, on 16 March 1818. [PAO.ms154]

QUAN, MICHAEL, a soldier of the 2nd Battalion of the 84th [Royal Highland Emigrants] Regiment, aboard the frigate Raleigh bound from New York to Charleston, South Carolina, in 1780. [NRS.GD174.2405]

RAWDON-HASTINGS, FRANCIS, an Irish officer in the British Army, raised the 'Volunteers of Ireland' Regiment in

Philadelphia, Pennsylvania, in 1777 which was later known as the 105th Regiment of Foot

RAYMOND, Lieutenant of the 18th [Royal Regiment of Ireland] Foot around 1770. [PEF.175]

REID, MAYNE, born 1818 in Ballyroney, County Down, fought in the Mexican War of 1840s and 1850s, later a journalist in New York and London, letters 1865 to 1883. [PRONI.D2802]

REILLY, BERNARD, late Colonel of Lord Digby's Regiment in Flanders, later in England, was bound for Jamaica in 1660. [SPAWI.1660.2016]

REYNOLDS, DANIEL, a soldier stationed at Placentia, Newfoundland, in 1732. [TNA.CO194.24.109]

REYNOLDS, JAMES, a soldier of the 18th [Royal Regiment of Ireland] Foot in New York in 1775. [TNA.WO.76/25]

RICHARDS, EDWARD, a Captain Lieutenant of the 55th [Westmorland] Regiment in St Lucia, a will dated 1798. [PWI]

RICHARDSON, Lieutenant JAMES, of the 18th [Inniskilling] Foot, was promoted to be Captain Lieutenant in place of Thomas Searle on 19 January 1782. [SM.44.55]

RICHARDSON, WILLIAM, Captain or Captain Lieutenant of the 18th [Royal Regiment of Ireland] Foot, was wounded at Bunker Hill, Massachusetts, in 1775; was promoted to be Major of the 104th [North British] Regiment on 17 September 1782 in place of Duncan Urquhart. [SM.44,504]

ROBERTS, JOSEPH, born 1727 in Ireland, a skinner in Augusta, Virginia, a soldier in Major Andrew Lewis's Company in Virginia in 1757. [VCS]

ROBERTSON, WILLIAM, from Dublin, a soldier in Dutch service, was aboard the White Swan bound from the Netherlands to the West Indies, an inventory, 1638. [ONA.Rot.Inv.293]

ROBINSON, JOHN, formerly a Major of Militia in Camden, South Carolina before the American Revolution, settled in Larne, Ireland, an affidavit, 1783. [TNA.AO.13.125.366-388]

ROCHE, Sir BOYLE, an officer at the Siege of Havanna, Cuba, in 1762, died in Dublin in 1807. [SM.69.479]

ROGERS, THOMAS, from Ireland to Maryland in 1772, settled in Ninety Six District, Craven County, South Carolina, a Loyalist Sergeant in the Ninety Six Militia, fought at King's Mountain and at Cowpens, returned to County Antrim, Ireland, by 1783, died there 10 September 1785. [TNA.AO12.46.355][UEL.II.1157]

ROSS, ROBERT, born 1766 in Dublin, Ireland, Lieutenant Colonel, of the 4th Royal Irish Dragoon Guards, was sent to Canada to stop American incursions there during the War of 1812, in 1814 he led an expeditionary force via the Battle of Bladensburg to Washington, D.C., which he captured and burnt, he then led his men towards Baltimore but was shot dead on 12 September 1814. He was buried in Halifax, Nova Scotia. [GM.88.368][UHF]

ROSS, WILLIAM, born 1769 in Ireland, settled on Cape Breton, Nova Scotia, by 1791, a Lieutenant of Militia, a petition in 1815. [NSARM.mf15792]

RUSSELL, JOHN, a soldier of the 18th [Royal Regiment of Ireland] Foot in Philadelphia, Pennsylvania, in 1767, died at Charleston Heights, Massachusetts, on 19 April 1775.   [TNA.WO.76/25; TNA.WO12.3501]

RUSSELL, JOHN, of the Grenadier Company of the 18th [Royal Regiment of Ireland] Foot, arrived in America in 1767, was killed at the Battle of Lexington, Massachusetts, in 1775. [PEF.23]

RUSSELL, PETER, born 1733, educated in Cork and at Cambridge University, fought as an officer of the 14th [Bedford] Regiment of Foot in the French and Indian War, later fought in the American War of Independence, by 1780 he was a Captain of the 64th [2nd Staffordshire] Regiment in the Leeward Islands, then was Judge of the Vice Admiralty Court in Charleston, South Carolina, from 1792 he was Receiver General in Canada, he died in 1809. [PRONI.mic.205.1]

RUSHTON, WILLIAM, a soldier of the 18th [Royal Regiment of Ireland] Foot, in New York in 1775. [TNA.WO.76/25]

RYAN, FRANCIS, born 1734 in Ireland, a butcher in Amelia County, Virginia, enlisted in September 1755 in Captain David Bell's Company in Virginia. [VCS]

RYAN, SIMON, a soldier stationed at Placentia, Newfoundland, in 1732. [TNA.CO194.24.109]

ST GEORGE, MANSERGH, died in Ireland during 1790 of a wound received at the Battle of Germantown in Pennsylvania on 4 October 1777. [SM.52.464]

SANDERSON, JOHN, born in Ireland, a Loyalist soldier, settled in Nova Scotia by 1785. [TNA.AO12.49.141]

SAVAGE, GEORGE, a soldier of the 18th [Royal Regiment of Ireland] Foot, in Philadelphia, Pennsylvania, in 1770, died on 22 August 1770. [TNA.WO.76/25]

SAVAGE, PATRICK, an Ensign of the French Infantry, embarked on The Dauphine bound for Louisiana in 1718. [NWI.I.476-477]

SAVAGE, General PATRICIO, Corregidor of Huamanga, Peru, in 1769. [ISE.286]

SAYER, Lieutenant JOHN, of the 18th [Royal Regiment of Ireland] Foot, was promoted to be Captain of the 89th [Princess Victoria's] Foot on 2 November 1779. [SM.41.632]

SCOTT, WALTER, was born in Ireland, emigrated to America in 1765, settled at Stillwater, New York, he and his sons enlisted with General Burgoyne, later moved to Isle Aux Noix, Montreal, by 1783. [OBA]

SCULLY, PHILLIP, a militiaman in Captain William Allanby's Company on Barbados in 1679. [H2.153]

SCURLOCK, THOMAS, probably from Dublin, a soldier who was admitted as a freeman of New York in 1702, later a vintner there, probate 1747, New York.

SEARLE, Captain Lieutenant THOMAS, of the 18th [Inniskilling] Foot, was promoted to Captain in place of George Bewes, on 26 January 1782. [SM.44.55]

SEBRIGHT, Sir JOHN SAUNDERS, Major General of the 18th [Royal Regiment of Ireland] Foot in 1762, Field Officer of the same regiment around 1770, Colonel, in Philadelphia, Pennsylvania, on 31 October 1772; in New York in 1777, died on 23 February in 1794. [TNA.WO.76/25; WO.12.3501 [PEF.85]

SERGEANT, HUGH, a Sergeant of the 18th [Royal Regiment of Ireland] Foot in Philadelphia, Pennsylvania, in 1767. [TNA.WO.76/25; WO.12.3501]

SERLE, THOMAS, Ensign or Volunteer of the 18th [Royal Regiment of Ireland] Foot around 1770. [PEF.192]

SHANLEY, MICHAEL, in Killashee, County Longford, an army pensioner, applied to settled in Canada on 17 March 1827. [TNA.CO384.16]

SHANNON, SAMUEL, a soldier of the 18th [Royal Regiment of Ireland] Foot in Philadelphia, Pennsylvania, in 1767. [TNA.WO.76/25]

SHARPLES, EDWARD, a soldier of the 18th [Royal Regiment of Ireland] Foot, in New York, was transferred on 24 December 1774. [TNA.WO.76/25]; a soldier of the 18th Foot, at Charleston Heights, Massachusetts, in 1775. [TNA.WO12.3501]

SHAW, HENRY, Ensign or Volunteer of the 18th [Royal Regiment of Ireland] Foot around 1770. [PEF.193]

SHAW, JAMES, emigrated from Ireland to America in 1754, settled in New York, a Loyalist and a militiaman in New York, moved to Sorel, Canada, in 1783. [UEL.II.1208]

SHEA, JOHN, a soldier of the 2nd Battalion of the 84th [Royal Highland Emigrants] Regiment, aboard the frigate Raleigh bound from New York to Charleston, South Carolina, in 1780. [NRS.GD174.2405]

SHEE, JOHN, Field Officer of the 18th [Royal Regiment of Ireland] Foot around 1770, in Boston, New England, in 1774, Captain of the 18th Foot at Charleston Heights, Massachusetts, in 1775; Major of the 18th Foot was promoted to Lieutenant Colonel of the 58th [Rutlandshire] Foot on 30 October 1779. [SM.41.575][PEF.20/88][TNA.WO12.3501]

SHEE, ROBERT, Captain of the Dillon Regiment, of the Irish Brigade in French Service, in America between 1778 and 1783. [IS.XIII.51]

SHEE, WILLIAM, Sub Lieutenant of the Dillon Regiment, of the Irish Brigade in French Service, in America between 1778 and 1783. [IS.XIII.51]

SHEEHAN, TERRENCE, a soldier of the 2nd Battalion of the 84th [Royal Highland Emigrants] Regiment, aboard the frigate Raleigh bound from New York to Charleston, South Carolina, in 1780. [NRS.GD174.2405]

SHELDON, WILLIAM, Sub Lieutenant of the Dillon Regiment, of the Irish Brigade in French Service, in America between 1778 and 1783. [IS.XIII.51]

SHENEHAN, DERBY, a militiaman in Captain Timothy's Company on Barbados in 1679. [H2.80]

SHEWBRIDGE, JOSEPH, an officer of the Royal Irish Artillery, died in the West Indies in 1795. [IS.XVI]

SINGLETON, GEORGE, born in Ireland, settled in New York as a merchant, a Loyalist and officer of the King's Royal Regiment of New York during the American War, later settled in Fredericksburgh, died there in 1789. [DCB]

SKELLY, Captain, of the 71st [Highland] Regiment, in 1782. [HMC.American.iii.226]

SKENE, ..., a Captain of Lord Blakeney's Regiment, was wounded at the Siege of Ticonderoga, New York, in July 1758.

SLATOR, WILLIAM HENRY, Ensign or Volunteer of the 18TH [Royal Regiment of Ireland] Foot around 1770. [PEF.194]

SMITH, DARBY, a soldier of the 2nd Battalion of the 84th [Royal Highland Emigrants] Regiment, aboard the frigate Raleigh bound from New York to Charleston, South Carolina, in 1780. [NRS.GD174.2405]

SMITH, Dr GEORGE, emigrated from Ireland to America in 1770, settled at Fort Edward, New York, until 1775, a Loyalist and British Army surgeon, a Major of Jessop's Corps, moved to Canada by 1787. [OBA][UEL.I.365]

SMITH, JOHN, a soldier of the 18th [Royal Regiment of Ireland] Foot in Philadelphia, Pennsylvania, in 1772. [TNA.W0.76/25]

SMITH, ROBERT, in Dungannon, County Tyrone, late of the Loyal Yeomanry Volunteers, applied to settle in Canada on 16 May 1827. [TNA.CO384.16]

SMITH, SAMUEL, a soldier of the 27th [Inniskilling] Foot at Fort George, New York, on 4 September 1757. [NRS.GD45.2.35.2]

SMITH, STEPHEN, formerly of the Prince of York's Chasseurs, settled in Bathurst, Ontario, on 21 October 1819. [PAO.ms154]

SMITH, THOMAS, a grenadier, of the 18th [Royal Regiment of Ireland] Foot, was killed at the Battle of Bunker Hill, Massachusetts, in 1775. [PEF.23]

SMITH, THOMAS, a soldier of the 18th [Royal Regiment of Ireland] Foot in Philadelphia, Pennsylvania, in 1767; at Charleston Heights, Massachusetts, in 1775. [TNA.WO.76/25; TNA.WO12.3501]

SMITH, THOMAS, a soldier of the 18th [Royal Regiment of Ireland] Foot, was killed at Bunker Hill, Massachusetts, in 1775.

SMITH, WILLIAM, Lieutenant of the 18th [Royal Regiment of Ireland] Foot around 1770; Lieutenant of the 18th [Royal Regiment of Ireland] Foot in Philadelphia, Pennsylvania, in 1767. [TNA.WO.76/25][PEF.176]

SMITH, WILLIAM, Staff Officer of the 18th [Royal Irish Regiment] Foot around 1770. [PEF.217]

SMITH, WILLIAM, an officer of the Royal Irish Artillery, died in the West Indies on 29 March 1794. [IS.XVI]

SNOW, WILLIAM, brother of Robert Snow in Waterford city, Ireland, a prisoner-of-war in New York, letters in 1782. [NLI. Mansfield pp]

SORRELS, WILLIAM, a soldier of the 18th [Royal Regiment of Ireland] Foot in Charlestown Heights, Massachusetts, died on 17 June 1775. [TNA.WO.12.3801]

SPAN, THOMAS, a Captain of the British Army in New York, wills, 1763-1768. [PWI]

SPARHAM, THOMAS, served in the 27th [Inniskilling] Regiment during the French and Indian War, was at the Siege of Havana, Cuba, and at Martinique, surgeon's mate in 1762, in 1768 when in the 60th [Royal American] Regiment, was appointed to a military hospital in Pensacola, Florida, settled at Crown Point, New York, in 1773, then was a surgeon to Burgoyne's Army, a memorial in 1783. [TNA.AO12.33.103]

SPARROW, ROBERT, a soldier of the 18th [Royal Regiment of Ireland] Foot in Philadelphia, Pennsylvania, in 1767. [TNA.WO.76/25]; a soldier of the 18th Foot, [Royal Regiment of Ireland], at Charleston Heights, Massachusetts, in 1775. [TNA.WO12.3501]

SPENCE, JACOB, a soldier of the 18th [Royal Regiment of Ireland] Foot in Charlestown Heights, Massachusetts, in 1775. [TNA.WO.12.3801]

SPRATT, HUGH, formerly Quartermaster Sergeant of the Glengarry Fencibles, settled in Kettley, Ontario, on 26 June 1817. [PAO.ms154]

STACK, EDWARD, a Captain of the Walsh Regiment, of the Irish Brigade in French Service, in America between 1778 and 1783. [IS.XIII.51]

STAINFORTH, GEORGE, Captain or Captain Lieutenant of the 18th [Royal Regiment of Ireland] Foot around 1770. [PEF.138]

STANLEY, DANIEL, born 1730 in Ireland, a shoemaker who enlisted in Captain David Bell's Militia Company in Virginia, on 1 May 1756. [VCS]

STEELE, THOMAS, a soldier of the 18th [Royal Regiment of Ireland] Foot in Philadelphia in 1767.   [TNA.WO.76/25]

STEELE, WILLIAM, born 1717, emigrated from Ireland to Brunswick, New Jersey, in 1759, a planter there, a Loyalist soldier, in Cork, Ireland, by 1784. [TNA.AO1214.351]

STEVENSON, Dr HENRY, born in Ireland, a physician who emigrated to Baltimore, Maryland, in 1756, a Loyalist in 1776, a surgeon of Tarleton's British Legion, in Westminster by 1786. [TNA.AO12.6.278]

STEWART, JOHN, Captain or Captain Lieutenant of the 18th [Royal Regiment of Ireland] Foot around 1770. [PEF.141]

STEWART, Captain, of the 27th [Inniskilling] Regiment, see letter from Charles Ross in Cork to Henry Dundas date 30 June 1799. [NRS.GD51.18.306]

STILLMAN, WILLIAM, in Inniskilling, County Fermanagh, an army pensioner, applied to settled in Canada on 24 March 1827. [TNA.CO384.16]

STIRLING, ROBERT, Captain of the 18th [Royal Regiment of Ireland] Foot, died in Dublin on 3 March 1754. [SM.16.154]

STOKES, WILLIAM, a soldier of the 18th [Royal Regiment of Ireland] Foot in Philadelphia, Pennsylvania, in 1770, and in 1772. [TNA.W0.76/25]

STRAIN, WILLIAM, born 1708 in Ireland, a sawyer in Frederick, Virginia, enlisted in May 1755, a soldier of Colonel George Washington's Company in August 1757. [VCS]

STRANGE, PATRICK, Sub Lieutenant of the Dillon Regiment, of the Irish Brigade in French Service, in America between 1778 and 1783. [IS.XIII.51]

SULLIVAN, ANTHONY, a militiaman of Captain James Ely's Company in Barbados in 1679. [H2.177]

SULLIVAN, DANIEL, a militiaman in Captain John Sampson's Company on Barbados in 1679. [H2.79]

SULLIVAN, DENIS, a soldier of Captain Hall's Militia Company on Barbados in 1679. [TNA.CO1.44.47]

SULLIVAN, DENNIS, born 1732 in Ireland, a seaman who enlisted in Captain Thomas Cocke's Company in Port Royal, Virginia, on 14 September 1755. [VCS]

SULLIVAN, HUMPHREY, a militiaman in Colonel Christopher Lyne's Regiment in Barbados in 1679. [TNA.CO1.44.47]

SULLIVAN, JOHN, a soldier in Captain Harrison's Company on Barbados in 1679. [TNA.CO1.44.47]

SULLIVAN, General JOHN, in Providence, a letter dated 4 June 1778. [SM.40.482]

SULLIVAN, JOHN, from Ireland, formerly in the Royal Navy, settled in Drummond, Ontario, on 18 September 1817. [PAO.ms154]

SULLIVAN, MATHEW, a militiaman in Captain John Sampson's Company on Barbados in 1679. [H2.79]

SULLIVAN, OWEN, a soldier stationed at Placentia, Newfoundland, in 1732. [TNA.CO194.24.109]

SULLIVAN, Sergeant TEAGE, in Halfwaytree Division, St Kitts, on 7 February 1678. [TNA.CO1.42]

SULLIVAN, THOMAS, a soldier stationed at Placentia, Newfoundland, in 1732. [TNA.CO194.24.109]

SULLIVAN, TIMOTHY, born 1736 in Ireland, a wagonner who enlisted in Captain David Bell's Company of Militia in Virginia, on 12 May 1756. [VCS]

SULLIVAN, WILLIAM, from Ireland, late a private of the 58th [Rutlandshire] Regiment, settled in Drummond, Ontario, on 30 November 1818. [PAO.ms154]

SUPPLE, MORRIS, born 1730 in Ireland, a seaman who enlisted in Captain Thomas Cocke's Company in Norfolk, Virginia, in November 1755. [VCS]

SUTCLIFF, JAMES, a soldier of the 18th [Royal Regiment of Ireland] Foot in Philadelphia, Pennsylvania, in 1767; at Charleston Heights, Massachusetts, in 1775. [TNA.WO.76/25; WO.12.3501]

SUTTON, Sergeant EDMUND, of the 18th [Royal Regiment of Ireland] Foot in 1772. [PEF.15]

SWALES, JOSEPH, a soldier of the 18th [Royal Regiment of Ireland] Foot, in New York, died on 23 October 1774. [TNA.WO.76/25]

SWEENEY, OWEN, born 1782, late of the 2nd Garrison Battalion, applied to settle in Canada in 1827. [TNA.CO384.16]

SWIGNY, EDMOND, Second Lieutenant of the Dillon Regiment, of the Irish Brigade in French Service, in America between 1778 and 1783. [IS.XIII.51]

SWIGNY, PAUL, Captain of the Dillon Regiment, of the Irish Brigade in French Service, in America between 1778 and 1783. [IS.XIII.51]

SWINEY, TERENCE, born 1717 in Ireland, an Indian trader in Augusta, Virginia, a soldier in Major Andrew Lewis's Company in Virginia in 1757. [VCS]

TAAFE, CHRISTOPHER, Second Lieutenant of the Dillon Regiment, of the Irish Brigade in French Service, in America between 1778 and 1783. [IS.XIII.51]

TAAFE, LAURENCE, Captain of the Dillon Regiment, of the Irish Brigade in French Service, in America between 1778 and 1783. [IS.XIII.51]

TATE, SAMUEL, born 1731 in Ireland, a smith, enlisted as a soldier of the Second Company of Rangers in Virginia on 21 October 1755. [VCS]

TAYLOR, PETER, in Clough, County Down, an army pensioner, applied to settle in Canada on 31 May 1827. [TNA.CO384.16]

TENANT, DAVID, born in Ireland, served in the 29th [Worcester] Regiment for 10 years, then settled in the Ninety-Six District of South Carolina, a Sergeant in the Light Horse of South Carolina moved to County Antrim, Ireland, by 1788. [TNA.AO12.52.119]

THOMAS, DANIEL, Staff Officer of the 18th [Royal Regiment of Ireland] Foot, Chaplain of the 18th Foot in 1770. [TNA.WO.76/25] [PEF.219]

THOMAS, JAMES, born 1736 in Ireland, a planter, enlisted in Captain David Bell's Company in Virginia on 22 April 1756. [VCS]

THOMASSON, THOMAS, Staff Officer of the 18th [Royal Regiment of Ireland] Foot around 1770, regimental surgeon in 1768, surgeon of the 18th Foot in 1770. [TNA.WO.76/25][PEF.220]

THOMPSON, JAMES, born in Ireland, served in the Royal Navy during the French and Indian Wars, settled in Philadelphia, Pennsylvania, before 1776, in 1781 he served aboard HMS London. [TNA.AO12100.63]

THOMPSON, JOHN, a soldier of the 18th [Royal Regiment of Ireland] Foot in Philadelphia, Pennsylvania, in 1767, in Charleston, Heights, Massachusetts, in 1775 [TNA.WO.76/75]

THOMPSON, JOHN, a former soldier of the 8th [The King's] Regiment, settled in Burgess, Ontario, on 22 August 1816. [PAO.ms154]

THOMPSON, JOHN, a private soldier in the 1st U. S. Artillery, two letters to his father Robert Thompson in County Londonderry, one re the Siege of Fort Sumner, South Carolina. [PRONI.T1585]

THOMPSON, WILLIAM, settled in the Ninety-Six District of South Carolina, a Loyalist militiaman, settled in Ballymena, County Antrim, Ireland, by 1784. [TNA.AO12.51.243]

THOMPSON, WILLIAM, emigrated from Ireland to America in 1764, settled as a spinning wheel maker in St George's parish, Georgia, joined the British Army after the Reduction of Savannah, moved via St Augustine and Antigua to England by 1785. [TNA.AO12.101.246]

THOMPSON, W. B., from Ireland, late of the Royal Sappers, settled in Dalhousie, Ontario, on 4 September 1820. [PAO.ms154]

THOMSON, ..., of the Volunteers of Ireland Regiment, was wounded in South Carolina in 1780. [SM.42.488]

THORNHILL, ROBERT, an officer of the Royal Irish Artillery from 1793 until 1795, a Major of the Royal Artillery in 1805, brevet Lieutenant Colonel in 1812, a Colonel in 1825, he died in Jamaica on 28 August 1825. [IS.XVI]

TOBIN, JAMES, a Second Lieutenant of the Walsh Regiment, of the Irish Brigade in French Service, in America between 1778 and 1783. [IS.XIII.51]

TONGE, WINCKWORTH, born 1728 in County Wexford, an Ensign of the 45th [Nottinghamshire] Regiment of Foot at Louisbourg from 176 until 1749, a Lieutenant in 1755, fought at the Sieges of Louisbourg and of Quebec in 1758-1759, later a politician and landowner in Nova Scotia, died in 1792. [DCB]

TONYN, CHARLES, Colonel of the 6th [Inniskilling] Dragoons, father of Patrick Tonyn, born 1725 in Berwick on Tweed, an officer of the Inniskilling Dragoons, Colonel of the 104th [North British] Regiment in 1761, Governor of East Florida from 1774 until 1784, Colonel of the 48th [Northamptonshire] Foot from 1787, died in London in 1804. [JCTP.87.4/14]

TOWELL, Lieutenant JOHN, of the 27th [Inniskilling] Foot, was promoted to Captain of the said regiment on 25 March 1777. [SM.39.168]

TRACEY, GODFREY, Ensign or Volunteer of the 18th [Royal Regiment of Ireland] Foot around 1770. [PEF.195]

TRAUT, THOMAS, a Second Lieutenant of the Walsh Regiment, of the Irish Brigade in French Service, in America between 1778 and 1783. [IS.XIII.51]

TRIMNIG, TEAGUE, a soldier in Captain Liston's Company on Barbados in 1679. [TNA.CO1.44.47]

TRIST, NICHOLAS, Lieutenant of the 18th [Royal Regiment of Ireland] Foot around 1770. [PEF.176]

TROY, SIMON, born 1736 in Ireland, a shoemaker in Essex Virginia, a soldier of Captain Henry Woodward's Company in Virginia, on 11 September 1757. [VCS]

TRULY, PETER, born 1730 in Ireland, a seaman who enlisted in Captain Thomas Cocke's Company in Norfolk, Virginia, on 6 July 1755. [VCS]

TUDER, THOMAS, born 1732 in Ireland, enlisted in Captain Christopher Gist's Company in Baltimore, Maryland, on 16 March 1756. [VCS]

TURNBULL, ALEXANDER, born 1721 in Ireland, enlisted in Captain Christopher Gist's Company in Lancaster, Pennsylvania, on 7 January 1756. [VCS]

TURNER, ALEXANDER, possibly from Newry, County Down, Ireland, settled at Rocky Creek, South Carolina, was killed in action at Winsborough, S.C. in February 1781. [TNA.AO12.52.355]

TURNER, SAMUEL, Staff Officer of the 18th [Royal Regiment of Ireland] Foot around 1770. [PEF.222]

TURNLEY, EDWARD, in 5 Brown Street, Belfast, late of the 72nd [Dule of Albany's Highlanders Regiment] Foot, applied to settle in Canada in 1827. [TNA.CO384.16]

TWENTYMAN, SAMUEL, Ensign or Volunteer of the 18th [Royal Regiment of Ireland] Foot around 1770. [PEF.196]

TYRELL, ARTHUR, an officer of the Royal Irish Artillery, died in the West Indies on 1 May 1794. [IS.XVI]

TYRELL, JAMES, in 33 Denzille Street, Dublin, served for 14 years in the 31st [Huntingdonshire] Regiment, applied to settle in Canada on 5 July 1827. [TNA.CO384.16]

TYRELL, JOHN, a supernumery of the 18th [Royal Regiment of Ireland] Foot in Philadelphia, Pennsylvania, on 27 October 1767; a soldier of the 18th Regiment, in Charlestown Heights, Massachusetts, in 1775. [TNA.WO.76/25; TNA.WO.12.3501]

VAUGHAN, JOHN, formerly a Captain of the 17th [The Loyal Irish] Regiment of Foot, late from America, died in Portarlington, Ireland, in January 1763. [FDJ.3725]

WADE, NICHOLAS, Captain of the 49th [Hertfordshire] Regiment, was promoted to Major of the 27th [Inniskilling] Foot in place of Michael Cuffe on 9 March 1779. [SM.41.222]

WAKEFIELD, HENRY, served in the 18th Regiment of Dragoons during the French and Indian War, then settled in York County, Pennsylvania, a Loyalist in London by 1784. [TNA.AO12.42.374]

WALKER, JAMES, settled on Cuffy Town Creek, Ninety-Six District, South Carolina, a Loyalist soldier, later in Ballymore, northern Ireland, by 178- [TNA.AO.12.46.220]

WALKER, JOHN, drummer of the 18th [Royal Regiment of Ireland] Foot in Philadelphia, Pennsylvania, in 1767. [TNA.WO.76/25]

WALKER, JOHN, in Dungannon, County Tyrone, late of the Loyal Yeomanry Volunteers, applied to settle in Canada on 16 May 1827. [TNA.CO384.16]

WALKER, ROBERT, a former Sergeant of the 27th [Inniskilling] Foot, in Kilmun on 16 November 1813. [NRS.CC2.8.117.7]

WALKER, 'STOFFEL', born 1615, from 'Wasloot' in Ireland, a soldier aboard the Neptunus bound from Delft in the Netherlands for the West Indies in 1637. [GAR.ONA.390.99.162]

WALL, PATRICK, a soldier of the 2nd Battalion of the 84th [Royal Highland Emigrants] Regiment, aboard the frigate Raleigh bound from New York to Charleston, South Carolina, in 1780. [NRS.GD174.2405]

WALL, WILLIAM, a soldier stationed at Placentia, Newfoundland, in 1732. [TNA.CO194.24.109]

WALLACE, JAMES, in Ballibaro, County Cavan, served for 10 years in the 29th [Worcester] Foot, applied to settle in Canada on 21 March 1827. [TNA.CO384.16]

WALLACE, THOMAS, a soldier of the 18th [Royal Regiment of Ireland] Foot in New York in 1775. [TNA.WO.76/25]

WALLACE, THOMAS, late private of the Glengarry Regiment, settled in Drummond, Ontario, on 18 July 1816. [PAO.ms154]

WALLACE, WILLIAM, emigrated from Ireland to America in 1773, settled at Long Cane, South Carolina, a Loyalist and militiaman until 1785, moved to Rawdon, Nova Scotia. [UEL.I.174]

WALSH, Brigadier General, commanding the 27th [Inniskilling] Regiment, captured Grenada in February 1762, also at the Siege of Havanna in June 1762, in 1765 the regiment was quartered in Quebec, Trois Rivieres, and Montreal, from 1767 until 1775 the 27th was based in Ireland, in 1776 the regiment returned to America. [IR.36/37]

WALSH, CHARLES, a Captain of the Walsh Regiment, of the Irish Brigade in French Service, in America between 1778 and 1783. [IS.XIII.51]

WALSH, HUNT, born 1720 at Ballykilcavan, Queen's County, Ireland, Colonel of the 28th [North Gloucestershire] Regiment, fought at Louisbourg and at the Plains of Abraham, was granted land on Prince Edward Island in 1767. [JCTP.74.413]

WALSH, PATRICK, born in Ireland, to America as a soldier of the 35th [Royal Sussex] Regiment in 1745, he was appointed as an Ensign and Adjutant in General Lyman's Regiment of Connecticut Provincials in 1751, later, was a Lieutenant of Colonel Eleazer Fitch's Provincial Regiment, he settled in New York City in 1763, during the Revolution he was a Captain of the King's American Rangers in Canada, moved to London by 1784. [TNA.AO12.24.260]

WALSH, WILLIAM, from Ireland, late of the Royal Sappers, settled in Lanark, Ontario, on 1 November 1820. [PAO.ms154]

WARBURTON, HUGH, born 1695, an officer of the 4th [King's Own] Regiment of Foot fought in the French and Indian War, later commander of the 27th [Inniskilling] Regiment of Foot, died in 1771.

WARD, JAMES, a super-numery of the 18th [Royal Irish Regiment] Foot, in Philadelphia, Pennsylvania, on 27 October 1767. [TNA.WO.76/25]

WARREN, L., Captain of the 27th [Inniskilling] Regiment, embarked for the West Indies in September 1796, fought at the Siege of Morne Fortune, St Lucia. [IR.154]

WATSON, ANDREW, a Captain of the 27th [Inniskilling] Regiment, a disposition by his wife Elizabeth Watson on 11 January 1786. [NRS.GD109.1385]

WATSON, JOHN, in Tullycorbet, Ballibay, for 20 years in the 5th Dragoon Guards, applied to settle in Canada on 13 April 1827. [TNA.CO384.16]

WATSON, WILLIAM, in Venagh, County Tipperary, late Lieutenant of the 50th [Queen's Own] Regiment, applied to settle in Canada on 17 April 1827. [TNA.CO384.16]

WATTS, THOMAS, born 1723 in Ireland, a saddle maker who was recruited for William Cox's Rangers in Virginia on 21 October 1755. [VCS]

WATTWOOD, GEORGE, deserted from the 60th [Royal American] Regiment in Frederickstown, Frederick County, Maryland, in August 1756. [MG.591]

WEBB, THOMAS, born 1724, an army officer in America and the West Indies during the French and Indian War 1756-1763, he fought at Louisbourg and at Quebec, from 1764 until 1775 he was a Lieutenant of the 120th Regiment on the Irish Establishment, and Barrack Master at Albany, New York, he moved to London in 1778. [TNA.AO12.24.342]

WEIR, CHRISTOPHER, enlisted in Ireland was captured with Lieutenant North's detachment of the 33rd [McDonald's Regiment] Foot at Saratoga, was imprisoned for four years but escaped. [HMC.American.iii.287]

WELCH, JOHN, born 1721 in Ireland, a labourer in Baltimore, Maryland, a soldier in Captain Robert Spotswood's Company at Fort Young in 1757. [VCS]

WELSH, EDWARD, a militiaman in Barbados in 1679. [TNA.CO1.44.47]

WELSH, GEORGE, in Castle Billingham, County Louth, late of the 82nd [Prince of Wales Volunteers] Regiment, applied to settle in Canada on 25 April 1827. [TNA.CO384.16]

GREENLAW, MICHAEL, Lieutenant of the Dillon Regiment, of the Irish Brigade in French Service, in America between 1778 and 1783. [IS.XIII.51]

WHATLEY, ..., of the Volunteers of Ireland Regiment, was wounded in South Carolina in 1780. [SM.42.488]

WHEATLET, ROBERT, in Kilbride, County Carlow, for 24 years in the 39th [Dorset] Foot, applied to settle in Canada in 10 July 1839. [TNA.CO384.16]

WHEELOCK, ANTHONY, Captain of the 27th [Inniskilling] Regiment, in 1747, in Massachusetts and New Hampshire in 1759, and New York in 1760. [ARS.20]

WHITE, JOHN, a soldier of the 18th [Royal Regiment of Ireland] Foot, in New York in 1775. [TNA.WO.76/25]

WHITE, ALEXANDER, born in Ireland, emigrated to America in 1756, settled in Tryon County, New York, a Loyalist barrack master in New York from 1778 until 1783, then moved to Sorrell via Quebec. [UEL.II.967]

WHITE, JOHN, a former Sergeant of the 70th [Surrey] Regiment, settled in Bathurst, Ontario, on 2 September 1819. [PAO.ms154]

WHITLEY, CHARLES DAVYS, an Ensign of the Volunteers of Ireland Regiment, died of wounds received at the Battle of Camden, South Carolina, on 16 August 1780, a warrant to pay his widow Elizabeth Whitley, dated 28 August 1782. [HMC.American.iii.97]

WILCOCKS, JOHN, Ensign or Volunteer of the 18th [Royal Regiment of Ireland] Foot around 1770. [PEF.197]

WILKINS, JOHN, FOLLIOT, Field Officer of the 18th [Royal Regiment of Ireland] Foot around 1770, a Lieutenant Colonel in Philadelphia, Pennsylvania, in 1768. [PEF.92]

WILKINS, THOMAS, born 1712, MD, 'it was in his arms the +immortal Wolfe breathed his last after Quebec had surrendered to His Majesty's Forces on 18 June 1759', died in Galway in 1814. [SM.76.400]

WILKINSON, JOHN, a soldier of the 18th [Royal Regiment of Ireland] Foot in Philadelphia, Pennsylvania in 1770, was transferred on 9 October 1774 in New York. [TNA.WO.76/25; WO.12.3501]

WILKINSON, JOHN, in Randalstown, Ireland, late of the 45th [Nottinghamshire] Regiment and of the 13th Veteran Battalion, applied to settle in Canada on 24 December 1827. [TNA.CO384.16]

WILLIAMS, HENRY, born 1730 in Ireland, a Sergeant in Captain Thomas Cocke's Company, a planter who enlisted in Frederick, Virginia, on 21 July 1754. [VCS]

WILLIAMS, JOHN, a soldier of the 18th [Royal Regiment of Ireland] Foot in Philadelphia, Pennsylvania, in 1772, transferred to Lord's Company, in April 1771. [TNA.WO.76/25]

WILLIAMS, WILLIAM, a Corporal of the 18th [Royal Regiment of Ireland] Foot in Philadelphia, Pennsylvania, in 1767, a Sergeant at Charleston Heights, Massachusetts, in 1774, died 31 December 1774. [TNA.WO.76/25; WO.12.3501]

WILLIAMSON, ADAM, Field Officer of the 18th [Royal Regiment of Ireland] Foot around 1770. [PEF.99]

WILLIS, JOHN, from Ireland, formerly a Sergeant of the 59th [Nottinghamshire] Regiment, settled in Bathurst, Ontario, on 9 August 1817, later in Drummond, Ontario, on 20 May 1820. [PAO.ms154]

WILLISRAFT, WILLIAM, at Flurry Bridge, County Louth, a Sergeant of the Yeomanry for 30 years, applied to settle in Canada on 14 May 1827. [TNA.CO384.16]

WILSON, JOHN, born 1696 in Galway, 5 feet 8 inches tall, a schoolmaster who deserted from Captain Robert Hodgson's Independent Company in 1746. [MG.27.6.1746]

WILSON, PATRICK, in Catharcamlish, Limerick, late of the 41st [Welch] Regiment, applied to settle in Canada on 16 April 1827. [TNA.CO384.16]

WILSON, RICHARD, born in Ireland, a soldier of the 22nd [Cheshire] Regiment during the French and Indian War, settled in Mecklenburg County, North Carolina, in 1771, a Lieutenant at Fort Johnstone, North Carolina, in 1775-1776, a Loyalist officer of the Royal Fencibles from 1775 until 1782. [UEL.II.1155] [TNA.WO17.124]

WILSON, WILLIAM, emigrated from Ireland to America in 1775, settled in South Carolina, a Loyalist Lieutenant of Militia, moved to London by 1785. [TNA.AO13.136.201]

WILTSHIRE, HENRY, born 1717 in Ireland, a coachmaker in Frederick, Virginia, enlisted in October 1756, a soldier in Colonel George Washington's Company in August 1757. [VCS]

WINN, THOMAS, born in Ireland, settled in Cherry Valley, New York, a Sergeant of Butler's Corps of Rangers during the American Revolution, settled at Niagara by 1783. [TNA.AO12.101.197]

WITHERS, alias DELANEY, WILLIAM, born 1722, deserted from the Maryland Forces at Fort Frederick in 1756. [MG.587]

WITHEY, JOHN, a soldier of the 18th [Royal Regiment of Ireland] Foot in Philadelphia, Pennsylvania, in 1772; in New York in 1775. [TNA.WO.76/25]

WOODS, JAMES, late private of the Glengarry Regiment, settled in Drummond, Ontario, on 16 July 1816. [PAO.ms154]

WRIGHT, JAMES, late of the Royal Sappers, settled in Lanark, Ontario, on 1 November 1820. [PAO.ms154]

WRIGHTSON, JOHN, a Captain of Lord Blakeney's Regiment, the 27th [Inniskilling] Foot, at Elizabethtown and Rimebeck in 1757, letters; he was wounded at the Siege of Ticonderoga, New York, in July 1758. [NRS.GD45.2.14.1-6]

WYNNE, LEWIS, Captain or Captain Lieutenant of the 18th [Royal Regiment of Ireland] Foot, died on 14 March 1771. [PEF.142]

YOBB, MOSES, in Cookstown, County Tyrone, 17 years' service in the Loughgall Yeomanry, applied to settle in Canada on 18 June 1827. [TNA.CO384.16]

YOUNG, GEORGE, from Ireland, late private of the 3rd [Kent] Regiment, settled in Oxford, Ontario, on 13 October 1817. [PAO.ms154]

YOUNG, JAMES, from Ireland, formerly a Sergeant of the 103rd Regiment, settled in Drummond, Ontario, on 22 June 1822. [PAO.ms154]

REFERENCES

ANY St Andrews Society of New York

ARS Army Record Society

BL British Library, London

CC Canadian Courant, series

DAL Dalton's English Army Lists, [London 1960]

FDJ Freeman's Dublin Journal, series

GAR Rotterdam Archives

HS Haykluyt Society, London

IR Historical Record of the 27th [Inniskilling] Regiment, [Enniskillen, 1878]

ISE Ireland and the Spanish Empire, [Dublin, 2010]

HMC Historic Manuscript Commission, London

ISPO Irish State Paper Office, Dublin

MG Maryland Gazette, series

NAM National Army Museum, London

NMM National Maritime Museum, Greenwich

NSARM Nova Scotia Archives Records Management

OBA Ontario Bureau of Archives

ONA.Rot. Rotterdam Archives

PAO Public Archives of Ontario113

PEF Protecting the Empire's Frontier, [Ohio, 2013]

PRO.I Public Record Office, Ireland

PWI Prerogative Wills of Ireland

RUSI Royal United Service Institution, London

SM Scots Magazine, series

TCD Trinity College, Dublin

TNA The National Archives, London

UHF Ulster Historical Foundation

VCS Virginia's Colonial Soldiers, [Baltimore, 1988]

www.ingramcontent.com/pod-product-compliance
Lightning Source LLC
Chambersburg PA
CBHW071512150426
43191CB00009B/1496